Popular Music Theory

Advanced Level
Grades 6 to 8

by

Camilla Sheldon & Tony Skinner

A CIP record for this publication is available from the British Library.

ISBN: 1-898466-46-7

First edition © 2001 Registry Publications Ltd.

Published in Great Britain by

Registry House, Churchill Mews, Dennett Rd, Croydon, Surrey, CR0 3JH

Text and music proofing by Alan C Robertson

Typesetting by

Take Note Publishing Limited, Lingfield, Surrey

Instrument photographs supplied by John Hornby Skewes Ltd.

Printed in Great Britain.

Contents

Introduction

This book is a guide for students wishing to take the London College of Music Grade Six, Grade Seven or Grade Eight examinations in Popular Music Theory.

As well as helping you to pass these examinations, the intention of this book is to summarise the theory behind popular music and so help you improve your musicianship. You will benefit most if you try out the information you learn in this book in a practical music-making setting, by relating the information to your instrument and by using it to create your own music.

This book is part of a series that offers a structured and progressive approach to understanding the theory of popular music and whilst it can be used for independent study, it is ideally intended as a supplement to group or individual tuition.

The chapters of the book follow the sections of the examination. Each chapter outlines the facts you need to know for the examination, together with a summary of the theory behind the facts. Each chapter is completed with some examples of the type of questions that will appear in the examination papers. The sample questions are intended to provide a clear guide as to the kind of questions that may be asked in the examination, however the list of questions is neither exclusive nor exhaustive. Once you've worked through the questions at the end of each section, you can check your answers by looking at the 'sample answers' in the back of the book.

As the requirements for each examination are cumulative, it is essential that you have a good knowledge of the requirements for the previous grades. If you are not already familiar with this material, it is recommended that you also study the preceding handbooks in this series.

musical terms

Sometimes there are two different names that can be used for the same musical elements. Also, the terminology that is widely used in N. America (and increasingly amongst pop, rock and jazz musicians in the U.K. and elsewhere) is different to that traditionally used in the U.K. and other parts of Europe.

A summary of the main alternative terms is shown below. In the examination you can use either version. In this book we generally use the terms shown in the left-hand column – as these are the ones that are more commonly used amongst popular music musicians.

whole note	=	semibreve
half note	=	minim
quarter note	=	crotchet
eighth note	=	quaver
sixteenth note	=	semiquaver
whole step	=	whole tone
half step	=	semitone
staff	=	stave
treble clef	=	G clef
bass clef	=	F clef
measures	=	bars
keynote	=	tonic
leger line	=	ledger line
flat 2nd, 3rd, 6th or 7th	=	minor 2nd, 3rd, 6th or 7th
flat 5th	=	diminished 5th
sharp 4th or 5th	=	augmented 4th or 5th

Section One – scales and keys

In this section of each exam you may be asked to write out and identify any of the required scales (and their key signatures).

Scale requirements for Grade Six

Scales with key signatures to the range of five sharps and five flats:

- major
- natural minor
- harmonic minor
- pentatonic major
- pentatonic minor
- blues scales: C, G, D, A, E, B, F, B♭, E♭, A♭ and D♭
- Dorian modal scales: D, A, E, B, F♯, C♯, G, C, F, B♭ and E♭.
- Mixolydian modal scales: G, D, A, E, B, F♯, C, F, B♭, E♭ and A♭.
- Lydian modal scales: F, C, G, D, A, E, B♭, E♭, A♭, D♭ and G♭.
- chromatic scale starting on any keynote

Scale requirements for Grade Seven

Scales in all keys:

- major
- natural minor
- harmonic minor
- pentatonic major
- pentatonic minor
- blues
- Dorian, Phrygian, Lydian and Mixolydian modal scales
- chromatic and whole tone scales starting on any keynote

Scale requirements for Grade Eight

All requirements from all previous grades, plus in all keys:

- Locrian modal scale
- jazz melodic minor scale
- altered scale
- Phrygian major modal scale
- Lydian ♭7 (Lydian dominant) modal scale
- whole/half and half/whole diminished scales starting on any keynote

So that scales learnt in theory can be used effectively in a practical way, you should be able to do the following:

- Write out, or identify, each scale using standard *music notation* (adding or identifying the key signature where appropriate). You may be asked to write the scales in the treble clef or the bass clef, either ascending or descending.

- Write out, or identify, the *scale spelling* of each scale.

In this chapter we explain the theory behind the new scale types that have been added for each grade. We also summarise how to construct the scale types that have been covered in the previous grades books, however, If you have difficulty in understanding any of the concepts used it is recommended that you refer to the previous books in this series.

scale construction

Major scales are constructed using the following pattern of whole steps (whole tones) and half steps (semitones):

W W H W W W H

Natural minor scales are constructed using this pattern of whole steps and half steps:

W H W W H W W

Pentatonic major scales are constructed by taking the 1st, 2nd, 3rd, 5th and 6th notes of the major scale.

Pentatonic minor scales are constructed by taking the 1st, 3rd, 4th, 5th and 7th notes of the natural minor scale.

Harmonic minor scales are constructed by taking the natural minor scale (with the same keynote) and raising the 7th note by a half step.

Blues scales are constructed by taking the 1st, 3rd, 4th, 5th and 7th notes of the major scale (with the same keynote), lowering the 3rd and 7th notes by a half step, and adding the flattened 5th note. This means that blues scales contain both the flattened 5th and perfect 5th notes.

Modal scales are constructed by taking an existing scale starting from a note other than the original keynote:

- The major scale starting from its 2nd degree becomes the *Dorian modal scale*.

- The major scale starting from its 4th degree becomes the *Lydian modal scale*.

- The major scale starting from its 5th degree becomes the *Mixolydian modal scale*.

- The major scale starting from its 1st degree can also be called the *Ionian modal scale*, however this term is rarely used in popular music and the term 'major scale' is generally preferred.

- The major scale starting from its 6th degree can also be a called the *Aeolian modal scale*, however in popular music this modal scale is more usually referred to as the 'natural minor' or 'relative minor' scale.

Chromatic scales are constructed using only half steps, so all twelve notes between any note and its octave are used in this scale.

scale notation

Here are examples of each of the scale types that you are required to know for the Grade Six exam. You can work out the notes for scales in other keys by referring to the information regarding scale construction given previously. To maintain the correct enharmonic spelling when notating certain scales, sometimes a half step above B may need to be written as B♯, and a half step above E may need to be written as E♯. Similarly, sometimes a half step below C may need to be written as C♭, and a half step below F as F♭. Certain scales use double sharps (indicated by '×') and double flats (indicated by '♭♭').

Natural signs (♮) may need to be used in some scales in order to 'cancel' unrequired ♯s or ♭s that occur either in the key signature or previously in the bar.

Notice that natural, pentatonic and harmonic minor scales share the key signature of their relative major keys (i.e. the major key that is one whole step and a half step higher). Blues scales use the key signature of the major key with the same keynote.

major scales

B major scale

D♭ major scale

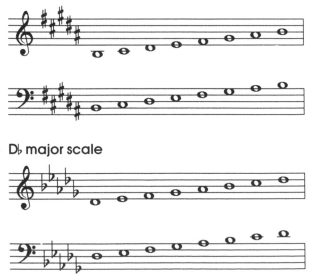

natural minor scales

G# natural minor scale

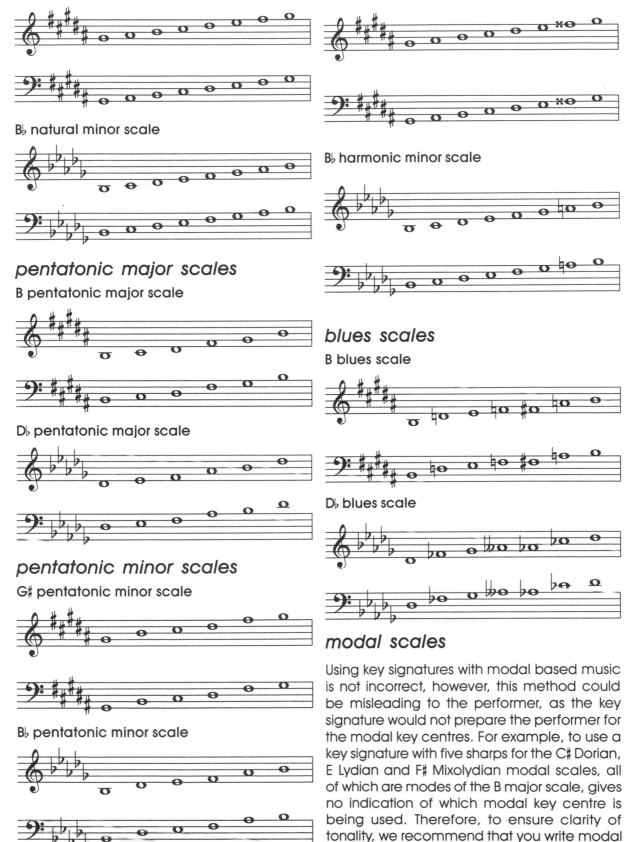

B♭ natural minor scale

pentatonic major scales

B pentatonic major scale

D♭ pentatonic major scale

pentatonic minor scales

G# pentatonic minor scale

B♭ pentatonic minor scale

harmonic minor scales

G# harmonic minor scale

B♭ harmonic minor scale

blues scales

B blues scale

D♭ blues scale

modal scales

Using key signatures with modal based music is not incorrect, however, this method could be misleading to the performer, as the key signature would not prepare the performer for the modal key centres. For example, to use a key signature with five sharps for the C# Dorian, E Lydian and F# Mixolydian modal scales, all of which are modes of the B major scale, gives no indication of which modal key centre is being used. Therefore, to ensure clarity of tonality, we recommend that you write modal scales, and music based on them, using accidentals rather than key signatures.

Here some examples of the Dorian, Lydian and Mixolydian modal scales.

Dorian modal scales

The Dorian modal scale is the mode that starts on the second degree of the major scale.

For example, C♯ is the 2nd note in the scale of B major, so the Dorian modal scale which is generated from the B major scale is the C♯ Dorian modal scale. The C♯ note becomes the keynote of the Dorian modal scale and the remaining notes in the B major scale make up the rest of the C♯ Dorian modal scale, as shown below.

C♯ Dorian modal scale

The E♭ Dorian modal scale contains the same notes as the D♭ major scale starting from its second degree, as shown below.

E♭ Dorian modal scale

Mixolydian modal scales

The Mixolydian modal scale is the mode that starts on the fifth degree of the major scale.

For example, F♯ is the 5th note in the scale of B major, so the Mixolydian modal scale which is generated from the B major scale is the F♯ Mixolydian modal scale. The F♯ note becomes the keynote of the Mixolydian modal scale and the remaining notes in the B major scale make up the rest of the **F♯ Mixolydian modal scale**, as shown in the following notation.

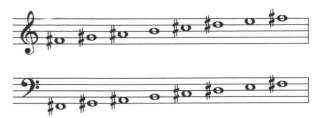

The **A♭ Mixolydian modal scale** contains the same notes as the D♭ major scale starting from its fifth degree, as shown below.

Lydian modal scales

The Lydian modal scale is the mode that starts on the fourth degree of the major scale.

For example, F is the 4th note in the scale of C major so the Lydian modal scale which is generated from the C major scale is the F Lydian modal scale. The F note becomes the keynote of the Lydian modal scale and the remaining notes in the C major scale make up the rest of the **F Lydian modal scale**, as shown below.

Here are two other examples of Lydian modal scales.

The **E Lydian modal scale** contains the same notes as the B major scale starting from its fourth degree, as shown below.

The G♭ **Lydian modal scale** contains the same notes as the D♭ major scale starting from its fourth degree, as shown below.

chromatic scales

In this book we explain how to notate the 'harmonic' chromatic scale (rather than the more obscure 'melodic' version). Each chromatic scale contains every half step between the starting note and the octave. When notating the (harmonic) chromatic scale it is standard practice to write only one letter name note for the keynote and fifth degree of the scale. For example, the chromatic scale starting on C would be written with only one type of C note (i.e. D♭ would be used, rather than C♯) and one type of G note (i.e. F♯ and A♭ would be used, rather than G♭ and G♯). There will then be two different notes for each other letter name. Notice the use of natural signs (♮) in cancelling unrequired ♯s and ♭s.

C chromatic scale

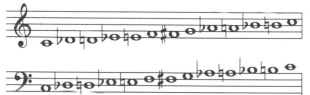

Here are some other examples of the chromatic scale. You should be able to write chromatic scales descending, as well as ascending. Because chromatic scales do not relate to any particular key, they should be written using accidentals rather than a key signature. The use of accidentals will vary with the direction of the scale.

G chromatic scale

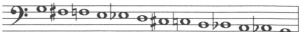

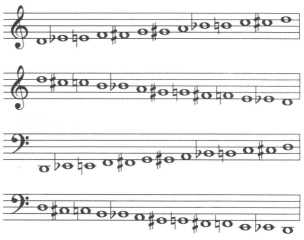

D chromatic scale

scale spellings

In popular music, musicians often use numbers to describe scales. This is called the *scale spelling*. Each note of the scale is given a number, starting with the keynote as '1'. Scale spellings are a useful and easy way to compare different scale types. Major scales are numbered as follows: 1 2 3 4 5 6 7 8

All other scale types are numbered in comparison to the major scale. If a number has a flat sign before it this means that the interval between it and the keynote is one half step smaller than the corresponding interval in a major scale. If the number has a sharp before it this means that the interval between it and the keynote is one half step larger than the corresponding interval in a major scale.

Here are the scale spellings you are required to know for the Grade Six exam.

Major scale:	1 2 3 4 5 6 7 8
Natural minor scale:	1 2 ♭3 4 5 ♭6 ♭7 8
Pentatonic major scale:	1 2 3 5 6 8
Pentatonic minor scale:	1 ♭3 4 5 ♭7 8
Harmonic minor scale:	1 2 ♭3 4 5 ♭6 7 8
Blues scale:	1 ♭3 4 ♭5 5 ♭7 8
Dorian modal scale:	1 2 ♭3 4 5 6 ♭7 8
Lydian modal scale:	1 2 3 ♯4 5 6 7 8
Mixolydian modal scale:	1 2 3 4 5 6 ♭7 8
Chromatic scale:	1 ♭2 2 ♭3 3 4 ♯4 5 ♭6 6 ♭7 7 8

The intervals between the keynote and the 2nd, 3rd, 6th and 7th notes in a major scale are known as *major* intervals. When these intervals are reduced by a half step they are known as *flattened* (or, if preferred, *minor*) intervals. For example, the Dorian modal scale contains a flattened 3rd interval (between the keynote and the third note in the scale) and a flattened 7th interval (between the keynote and seventh note in the scale).

The intervals between the keynote and the 4th and 5th notes in a major scale are known as *perfect* intervals. When these intervals are increased by a half step they are known as *sharpened*, *raised* or *augmented* intervals. (All three terms mean the same thing and are interchangeable, although consistency in use is advised). When the fifth interval is reduced by a half step it is known as a *flattened* (or, if preferred, *diminished*) fifth interval.

Sometimes it is also useful to compare scales of a minor tonality to the natural minor scale.

The natural minor scale is spelt: 1 2 ♭3 4 5 ♭6 ♭7 8
The pentatonic minor scale is the same as the natural minor scale but omitting the 2nd and 6th notes.
The harmonic minor scale is the same as the natural minor scale but with a major 7th interval (rather than a flattened 7th interval) between the keynote and the 7th note.
The Dorian modal scale is the same as the natural minor scale but with a major 6th interval (rather than a flattened 6th interval) between the keynote and the 6th note.

grade seven

As the requirements for each exam grade are cumulative it is essential that you thoroughly understand the requirements of the previous grades. It is particularly recommended that you revise the scale construction and scale spelling information given in the Grade Six section of this chapter before proceeding.

scale notation

Here are some examples of each of the scale types and keys that have been added for the Grade Seven exam. Notice how the key signatures containing six sharps or six flats are written. (Although it is possible to have key signatures with seven sharps or flats, these are used so rarely in popular music that they are not included in this book and series of exams).

In most of the examples below, the two scales given for each scale type are of the same pitch, although they use different enharmonic naming.

major scales

F♯ major scale.

G♭ major scale.

natural minor scales

D# natural minor scale.

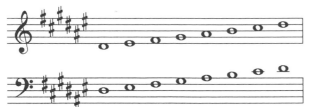

E♭ natural minor scale.

pentatonic major scales

F# pentatonic major scale.

G♭ pentatonic major scale.

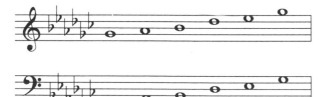

pentatonic minor scales

D# pentatonic minor scale.

E♭ pentatonic minor scale.

harmonic minor scales

D# harmonic minor scale.

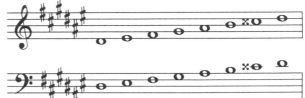

E♭ harmonic minor scale.

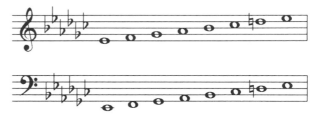

blues scales

F# blues scale.

G♭ blues scale.

chromatic scales

F# chromatic scale.

G♭ chromatic scale.

Dorian modal scales

G# Dorian modal scale.

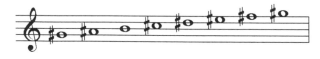

A♭ Dorian modal scale.

Lydian modal scales

B Lydian modal scale.

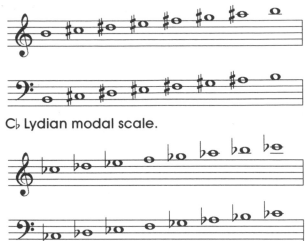

C♭ Lydian modal scale.

Mixolydian modal scales

C# Mixolydian modal scale.

D♭ Mixolydian modal scale.

Phrygian modal scales

The Phrygian modal scale is the mode that starts on the third degree of the major scale. For example, E is the 3rd note in the scale of C major so the Phrygian modal scale which is generated from the C major scale is the E Phrygian modal scale. The E note becomes the keynote of the Phrygian modal scale and the remaining notes in the C major scale make up the rest of the E Phrygian modal scale, as shown overleaf.

E Phrygian modal scale.

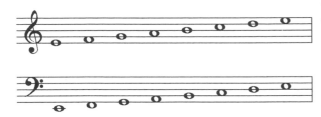

Here are two other examples of the Phrygian modal scale.

The A♯ Phrygian modal scale contains the same notes as the F♯ major scale starting from its third degree, as shown below.

A♯ Phrygian modal scale.

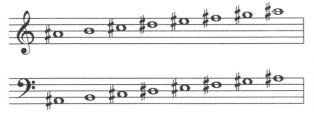

The B♭ Phrygian modal scale contains the same notes as the G♭ major scale starting from its third degree, as shown below.

B♭ Phrygian modal scale.

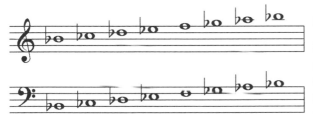

whole tone scales

Whole tone scales are constructed using only whole steps. Between any note and its octave there are six whole steps, therefore the whole tone scale contains six different notes. Because whole tone scales do not relate to any particular key, they should be written using accidentals rather than key signatures.

Here are two examples of the whole tone scale.

Whole tone scale starting from C.

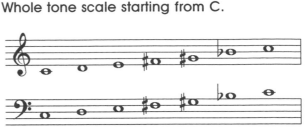

Whole tone scale starting from D♭.

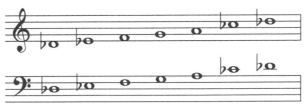

The enharmonic spelling used for the whole tone scale, particularly the use of the ♭7 rather than ♯6, is that which most accurately reflects its relationship to the dominant 7th♯5 chord (with the same starting note) – the chord with which it is most commonly used. However, when notating whole tone scales in the exam, any other systematic method of enharmonic spelling will be acceptable – providing its usage is consistent.

scale spellings

Here are the scale spellings for the scale types added at Grade Seven. The scale spellings of all the other types of scales required for Grade Seven are covered in the Grade Six section of this book.

Phrygian modal scale

1 ♭2 ♭3 4 5 ♭6 ♭7 8

As the Phrygian modal scale has a minor tonality, it is also useful to note that the Phrygian modal scale is the same as the natural minor scale but with a flattened 2nd.

whole tone scale

1 2 3 ♯4 ♯5 ♭7 8

As the requirements for each exam grade are cumulative it is essential that you thoroughly understand the requirements of the previous grades. It is particularly recommended that you revise the scale construction and scale spelling information given in the Grades Six and Seven sections of this chapter before proceeding.

scale notation

Here is a summary of the theory behind the additional scale types that have been added for the Grade Eight exam, as well as examples of each additional scale type.

Locrian modal scale

The Locrian modal scale is the mode that starts on the seventh degree of the major scale. For example, B is the 7th note in the scale of C major, so the Locrian modal scale which is generated from the C major scale is the B Locrian modal scale. The B note becomes the keynote of the Locrian modal scale and the remaining notes in the C major scale make up the rest of the B Locrian modal scale, as shown below.

B Locrian modal scale.

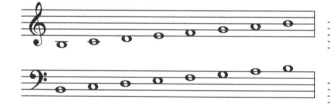

Here are two other examples of the Locrian modal scale.

The E♯ Locrian modal scale contains the same notes as the F♯ major scale starting from its seventh degree, as shown below.

E♯ Locrian modal scale.

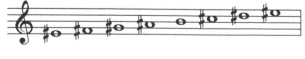
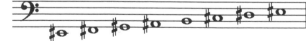

The F Locrian modal scale contains the same notes as the G♭ major scale starting from its seventh degree, as shown below.

F Locrian modal scale.

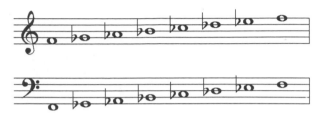

Phrygian major modal scale

Modal scales can be generated from scales other than the major scale. The Phrygian major modal scale starts on the fifth degree of the harmonic minor scale.

For example, G is the 5th note in the scale of C harmonic minor so the Phrygian major modal scale which is generated from the C harmonic minor scale is the G Phrygian major modal scale. The G note becomes the keynote of the Phrygian major modal scale and the remaining notes in the C harmonic minor scale make up the rest of the G Phrygian major modal scale, as shown below.

G Phrygian major modal scale.

Here are two other examples of the Phrygian major modal scale.

The F Phrygian major modal scale contains the same notes as the B♭ harmonic minor scale starting from its fifth degree, as shown below.

F Phrygian major modal scale.

The D# Phrygian major modal scale contains the same notes as the G# harmonic minor scale starting from its fifth degree, as shown below.

D# Phrygian major modal scale.

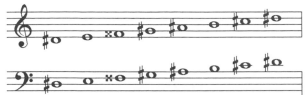

jazz melodic minor scale

The jazz melodic minor scale is constructed by taking the natural minor scale (with the same keynote) and raising the 6th and 7th notes by a half step. It is known as the 'jazz' melodic minor to distinguish it from the traditional 'classical' melodic minor scale which is rarely used in popular music (and which uses the notes of the natural minor scale when descending).

The C jazz melodic minor scale is written as follows:

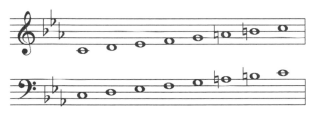

Here are two other examples of the jazz melodic minor scale.

D# jazz melodic minor.

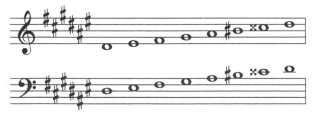

E♭ jazz melodic minor.

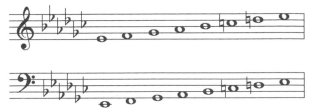

Lydian ♭7 modal scale

The Lydian ♭7 modal scale (also known as the Lydian dominant scale) is the modal scale which starts on the fourth degree of the jazz melodic minor scale.

For example, F is the 4th note in the scale of C jazz melodic minor, so the Lydian ♭7 modal scale which is generated from the C jazz melodic minor scale is the F Lydian ♭7 modal scale. The F note becomes the keynote of the Lydian ♭7 modal scale and the remaining notes in the C jazz melodic minor scale make up the rest of the F Lydian ♭7 modal scale, as shown below.

F Lydian ♭7 modal scale.

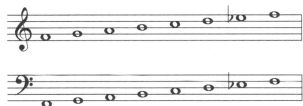

Here are two other examples of the Lydian ♭7 modal scale.

The B♭ Lydian ♭7 modal scale contains the same notes as the F jazz melodic minor scale starting from its fourth degree, as shown below.

B♭ Lydian ♭7 modal scale.

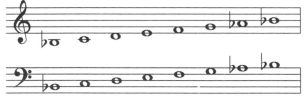

The G♯ Lydian ♭7 modal scale contains the same notes as the D♯ jazz melodic minor scale starting from its fourth degree, as shown below.

G♯ Lydian ♭7 modal scale.

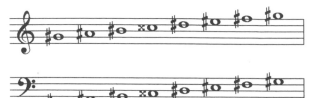

altered scale

The altered scale starts on the seventh degree of the jazz melodic minor scale.

For example, B is the 7th note in the scale of C jazz melodic minor, so the altered scale which is generated from this scale is the B altered scale. The B note becomes the keynote of the altered scale and the remaining notes in the C jazz melodic minor scale make up the rest of the B altered scale, as shown below.

Notice, however, that the enharmonic spelling used for notating the altered scale is that which most accurately reflects its relationship to the altered dominant 7th chords built on its keynote – the chord types with which it is most commonly used (e,g, 7♯11, 7♯5, 7♭9, 7♯9). The scale spelling used is 1 ♭2 ♯2 3 ♯4 ♯5 ♭7 8.

B altered scale.

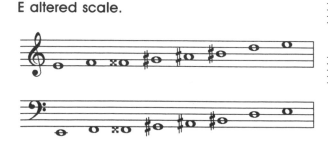

Here are two other examples of the altered scale.

E altered scale.

D♯ altered scale.

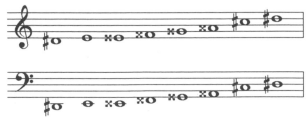

diminished scales

Diminished scales contain eight different notes and are made up of alternating whole step and half step intervals. Because diminished scales do not relate to any particular key, they should be written using accidentals rather than key signatures.

Diminished scales can start either with a whole step or a half step. Diminished scales that start with a whole step are described as *whole/half* diminished scales; diminished scales that start with a half step are described as *half/whole* diminished scales. Diminished scales are also described both as *symmetrical* scales, because of the regularity of the pattern, and *octatonic* scales, because each scale contains eight notes.

Here are some examples of the whole/half diminished scale.

Whole/half diminished scale, starting on C.

Whole/half diminished scale, starting on C♯.

Whole/half diminished scale, starting on D.

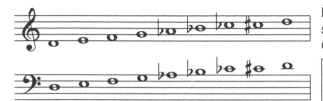

The enharmonic spelling used for the whole/half diminished scale is that which most accurately reflects its relationship to the diminished 7th chord built on its keynote – the chord with which it is most commonly used. However, when notating whole/half diminished scales in the exam, any other systematic method of enharmonic spelling will be acceptable – providing usage is consistent.

Here are some examples of the half/whole diminished scale.

Half/whole diminished scale, starting on C.

Half/whole diminished scale, starting on C♯.

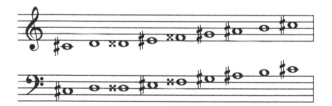

Half/whole diminished scale, starting on D.

The enharmonic spelling used for the half/whole diminished scale is that which most accurately reflects its relationship to the dominant 7th chord built on its keynote – the chord with which it is most commonly used. However, when notating half/whole diminished scales in the exam, any other systematic method of enharmonic spelling will be acceptable – providing usage is consistent.

scale spellings

Here are the scale spellings for the additional scale types that have been added for the Grade Eight exam.

Locrian modal scales:	1 ♭2 ♭3 4 ♭5 ♭6 ♭7 8
Phrygian major modal scales:	1 ♭2 3 4 5 ♭6 ♭7 8
Jazz melodic minor scales:	1 2 ♭3 4 5 6 7 8
Lydian ♭7 modal scales:	1 2 3 ♯4 5 6 ♭7 8
Altered scales:	1 ♭2 ♯2 3 ♯4 ♯5 ♭7 8
Whole/half diminished scales:	1 2 ♭3 4 ♭5 ♭6 ♭♭7 7 8
Half/whole diminished scales:	1 ♭2 ♯2 3 ♯4 5 6 ♭7 8

The scale spellings used for the whole tone, altered and diminished scales are those which most accurately reflect the relationship to the type of chords most commonly employed with them. When using their scale spellings in the exam, however, any other systematic method will be acceptable – providing usage is consistent.

comparing scales

To help you remember each type of scale it can be useful to compare scales with each other.

major scale:	1 2 3 4 5 6 7 8	G major:	G A B C D E F♯ G
pentatonic major:	1 2 3 5 6 8	G pentatonic major:	G A B D E G
natural minor:	1 2 ♭3 4 5 ♭6 ♭7 8	G natural minor:	G A B♭ C D E♭ F G
pentatonic minor:	1 ♭3 4 5 ♭7 8	G pentatonic minor:	G B♭ C D F G
harmonic minor:	1 2 ♭3 4 5 ♭6 7 8	G harmonic minor:	G A B♭ C D E♭ F♯ G
blues:	1 ♭3 4 ♭5 5 ♭7 8	G blues:	G B♭ C D♭ D F G
Dorian modal scale:	1 2 ♭3 4 5 6 ♭7 8	G Dorian scale:	G A B♭ C D E F G
Phrygian modal scale:	1 ♭2 ♭3 4 5 ♭6 ♭7 8	G Phrygian modal scale:	G A♭ B♭ C D E♭ F G
Lydian modal scale:	1 2 3 ♯4 5 6 7 8	G Lydian modal scale:	G A B C♯ D E F♯ G
Mixolydian modal scale:	1 2 3 4 5 6 ♭7 8	G Mixolydian modal scale:	G A B C D E F G
Locrian modal scale:	1 ♭2 ♭3 4 ♭5 ♭6 ♭7 8	G Locrian modal scale:	G A♭ B♭ C D♭ E♭ F G
Phrygian major modal scale:	1 ♭2 3 4 5 ♭6 ♭7 8	G Phrygian major modal scale:	G A♭ B C D E♭ F G
Jazz melodic minor:	1 2 ♭3 4 5 6 7 8	G jazz melodic minor:	G A B♭ C D E F♯ G
Lydian ♭7 modal scale:	1 2 3 ♯4 5 6 ♭7 8	G Lydian ♭7 modal scale:	G A B C♯ D E F G
Altered scale:	1 ♭2 ♯2 3 ♯4 ♯5 ♭7 8	G altered scale:	G A♭ A♯ B C♯ D♯ F G
Chromatic scale:	1 ♭2 2 ♭3 3 4 ♯4 5 ♭6 6 ♭7 7 8	G chromatic scale:	G A♭ A B♭ B C C♯ D E♭ E F F♯ G
Whole tone scale:	1 2 3 ♯4 ♯5 ♭7 8	G whole tone:	G A B C♯ D♯ F G
Whole/half diminished scales:	1 2 ♭3 4 ♭5 ♭6 ♭7 7 8	G whole/half diminished:	G A B♭ C D♭ E♭ F♭ F♯ G
Half/whole diminished scales:	1 ♭2 ♯2 3 ♯4 5 6 ♭7 8	G half/whole diminished:	G A♭ A♯ B C♯ D E F G

Alternatively, scales can also be compared directly with each other. For example:

- the Locrian modal scale is the same as the Phrygian modal scale, except for the interval between the keynote and the fifth note, which is flattened in the Locrian modal scale;

- the jazz melodic minor scale is the same as the major scale, except for the interval between the keynote and the third note, which is flattened in the jazz melodic minor scale;

- the Phrygian major modal scale, is the same as the Phrygian modal scale except for the interval between the keynote and the third note, which is a major third in the Phrygian major modal scale;

- the Lydian ♭7 modal scale is the same as the Mixolydian modal scale except for the interval between the keynote and the fourth note, which is sharpened in the Lydian ♭7 modal scale;

There follows some examples of the types of questions that candidates may be asked at Grades Six, Seven and Eight in this section of the exam. If you are unable to answer a question, then carefully re-read the preceding chapter. If necessary, refer to the preceding books in this series.

Use whole notes (semibreves) when answering a question that involves writing a scale in notation.

Sample questions for Grade Six

Q1. In the bass clef, write one octave ascending of the G♭ Lydian modal scale without using a key signature.

A1.

Q2. Using the correct key signature, write in the bass clef, one octave ascending of the harmonic minor scale that has five flats in the key signature.

A2.

Q3. In the treble clef, write one octave descending of the chromatic scale starting on D without using a key signature.

A3.

Q4. Using the correct key signature, write in the treble clef, one octave ascending of the pentatonic major scale that has five sharps in the key signature.

A4,

Q5. Write out the scale spellings for the following scales:

A5. Lydian modal scale: _____

Dorian modal scale: _____

Mixolydian modal scale: _____

Sample questions for Grade Seven

Q1. In the treble clef, write one octave descending of the D Phrygian modal scale without using a key signature.

A1.

Q2. In the treble clef, write one octave ascending of the G♯ Dorian modal scale without using a key signature.

A2.

Q3. In the bass clef, write one octave ascending of the whole tone scale starting from E without using a key signature.

A3.

Q4. Using the correct key signature write, in the bass clef, one octave ascending of the pentatonic minor scale that has six sharps in its key signature.

A4.

Q5. Write out the scale spellings for the following scales:

A5. Phrygian modal scale: _____

Blues scale : _____

Chromatic scale: _____

Sample questions for Grade Eight

Q1. In the treble clef, write one octave descending of the F Locrian modal scale without using a key signature.

A1.

Q2. In the bass clef, write one octave ascending of the E♭ Lydian ♭7 (E♭ Lydian dominant) modal scale without using a key signature.

A2.

Q3. In the treble clef, write one octave ascending of the G whole/half diminished scale without using a key signature.

A3.

Q4. Using the correct key signature write, in the bass clef, one octave ascending of the C♯ jazz melodic minor scale.

A4.

Q5. Write out the scale spellings for the following scales:

A5. Locrian modal scale: _____

Phrygian major modal scale: _____

Jazz melodic minor scale: _____

Section Two – chords

In this section of each exam you may be asked to write out and identify any of the chord types listed below.

Chord requirements for Grade Six

From major and natural minor scales within keys to the range of five sharps and five flats:

- all triads (major, minor, diminished, sus 2, sus 4 and 5th 'power' chords) in root position, and major, minor and diminished triads in 1st and 2nd inversion.
- major 7th, minor 7th, dominant 7th and minor 7th♭5 chords.
- major 6th and minor 6th chords.
- major 9th, minor 9th and dominant 9th chords.

From harmonic minor scales within keys to the range of five sharps and five flats:

- all triads (minor, diminished, augmented, major) in root position and 1st and 2nd inversion.
- minor/major 7th, minor 7th♭5, major 7th♯5, minor 7th , dominant 7th , major 7th and diminished 7th chords.

Chord requirements for Grade Seven

All the chord types listed for Grade Six with the range extended to *all* keys, plus:

- minor 11th and dominant 11th chords.
- major 13th, minor 13th and dominant 13th chords.
- dominant 7th and minor 7th chords with ♯ or ♭ 5ths.
- 1st, 2nd and 3rd inversions of major 7th, minor 7th and dominant 7th chords.

Chord requirements for Grade Eight

All chords listed in Grade Seven, plus (in all keys):

- dominant 7th chords with ♯ or ♭9ths
- minor 7th chords with ♭9ths
- major 7th and dominant 7th chords with ♯11ths
- commonly used altered bass 'slash chords'
- commonly used 'add chords'

So that the chords learnt in theory can be used effectively in a practical way, you should be able to do the following:

- Write out, or identify, the *chord symbol* of each chord.
- Write out, or identify, each chord using standard *music notation*. You may be asked to write your answers in either the treble clef or the bass clef.
- Write out, or identify, the *chord spelling* of each chord.

In this chapter we explain the theory behind the new chord types that have been added for each grade. We also summarise how to construct the chord types that have been covered in the previous grade books. However, if you have difficulty in understanding any of the concepts used it is recommended that you refer to the previous books in this series.

chord symbols

Here is a summary of the chord symbols for the main chord types set for Grades Six, Seven and Eight – written using C as the root of each chord. The chord symbols shown in the middle column are those most commonly used (and those recommended for use in the exam). A range of alternative symbols are sometimes used by pop musicians – the most commonly used of these are shown in the right hand column.

Major triad	C	Cma Cmaj
Minor triad	Cm	Cmi Cmin C-
Diminished triad	C°	Cdim
Augmented triad	C+	Caug
Sus2	Csus2	C2
Sus4	Csus4	C4
5th 'power chord'	C5	C5th
Major 7th	Cmaj7	Cma7 CM7 C△ C△7
Minor 7th	Cm7	Cmi7 Cmin7 C-7
Dominant 7th	C7	Cdom7
Minor 7th ♭5	Cm7♭5	C-7♭5 Cø Cmi7♭5 Cmin7♭5
Major 6th	C6	Cmaj6 Cma6 CM6
Minor 6th	Cm6	Cmi6 Cmin6 C-6
Major 9th	Cmaj9	CM9 Cma9
Minor 9th	Cm9	Cmi9 Cmin9 C-9
Dominant 9th	C9	Cdom9
Major/minor 7th	Cm/maj7	Cm△ Cm△7 C-△7
Major 7th ♯5	Cmaj7♯5	Cmaj7+5
Diminished seventh	C°7	Cdim7
Minor 11th	Cm11	Cmi11 Cmin11 C-11
Dominant 11th	C11	Cdom11
Major 13th	Cmaj13	CM13 Cma13
Minor 13th	Cm13	Cmi13 Cmin13 C-13
Dominant 13th	C13	Cdom13
Dominant 7th ♯5	C7♯5	C7+5 C+7 Cdom7♯5
Dominant 7th ♭5	C7♭5	Cdom7♭5
Minor 7th ♯5	Cm7♯5	Cm7+5 C-7♯5
C dominant 7th ♭9	C7♭9	Cdom7♭9
C dominant 7th ♯9	C7♯9.	C7+9 Cdom7♯9
C minor 7th ♭9	Cm7♭9	Cmi7♭9 Cmin7♭9 C-7♭9
C major 7th ♯11	Cmaj7♯11	Cmaj7+11 CM7♯11 C△♯11
C dominant 7th ♯11	C7♯11	C7+11 Cdom7♯11

Examples of chord symbols for inversions, 'slash chords' and 'add chords' are shown later in this chapter.

chord construction

Most triads are constructed by taking three alternate notes from a scale. The three notes become the root, third and fifth of the triad. There are four main types of triads constructed in this way: major, minor and diminished triads (from major, natural minor and harmonic minor scales) and augmented triads (from harmonic minor scales).

Major triads

- a major third interval between the root and the third

- a perfect fifth interval between the root and the fifth

Minor triads

- a flattened (minor) third interval between the root and the third

- a perfect fifth interval between the root and the fifth

Diminished triads

- a flattened (minor) third interval between the root and the third

- a flattened (diminished) fifth interval between the root and the fifth

Augmented triads

- a major third interval between the root and the third

- a sharpened (augmented) fifth interval between the root and the fifth

(A sharpened fifth interval is one half step larger than a perfect fifth interval.)

inversions

Chord inversions involve changing the order of notes within a chord from standard root position.

- 1st inversion is where the root is displaced from the bottom of the chord to the top, and the third becomes the lowest note.

- 2nd inversion is where the fifth becomes the lowest note.

Inversions have been covered in greater detail at Grade Five.

other triads

Variations of the basic triads that are required for this grade are shown below. More information about these variations can be found in earlier grade handbooks.

Sus 2 chords

- the third is replaced the second, i.e. by the note a whole step above the root.

Sus 4 chords

- the third is replaced by the fourth, i.e. by the note a whole step below the perfect fifth note.

5th 'power chords'

- the third is removed so that the chord consists of the root and the fifth. The octave is then (normally) added to give the chord a stronger sound.

chords built from major and natural minor scales

Some chords types are constructed by taking *four* alternate notes from a scale. The four notes become the root, third, fifth and seventh of the chord. The chord types constructed in this way from major and natural minor scales are: major 7th, minor 7th, dominant 7th and minor 7th♭5 chords. These are constructed as follows:

Major 7th chords

- a major third interval between the root and the third

- a perfect fifth interval between the root and the fifth

- a major seventh interval between the root and the seventh

Minor 7th chords

- a flattened (minor) third interval between the root and the third

- a perfect fifth interval between the root and the fifth

- a flattened (minor) seventh interval between the root and the seventh

Dominant 7th chords

- a major third interval between the root and the third
- a perfect fifth interval between the root and the fifth
- a flattened (minor) seventh interval between the root and the seventh

Minor 7th ♭5 chords

- a flattened (minor) third interval between the root and the third
- a flattened (diminished) fifth interval between the root and the fifth
- a flattened (minor) seventh interval between the root and the seventh

Some important variations of these chord types are shown below:

Major 6th chords

- a major third interval between the root and the third
- a perfect fifth interval between the root and the fifth
- a major sixth interval between the root and the sixth

Minor 6th chords

- a minor third interval between the root and the third
- a perfect fifth interval between the root and the fifth
- a major sixth interval between the root and the sixth

Ninth chords

Ninth chords are extensions of seventh chords – formed by adding the 9th note of the major scale with the same keynote. For example:

C major scale	C major 7th	C major 9th
C D E F G A B C D	C E G B	C E G B D
1 2 3 4 5 6 7 8 9	1 3 5 7	1 3 5 7 9

Any major 7th, minor 7th or dominant 7th chord can have a 9th chord extension added by using the 9th note of the major scale with the same keynote: minor 7th chords become minor 9ths, dominant 7th chords become dominant 9ths, and major 7th chords become major 9ths.

chords built from the harmonic minor scale

In the same way that triads and chords can be built from each degree of the major or natural minor scale, by using three or four alternate notes, triads and chords can also be built from each degree of the harmonic minor scale.

Here is the C harmonic minor scale with the triads that can be built in this way on each degree of the scale.

C harmonic minor scale	chord symbol	degree	chord tones
C D E♭ F G A♭ B C	Cm	I	C E♭ G
C D E♭ F G A♭ B C	D°	II	D F A♭
C D E♭ F G A♭ B C	E♭+	III	E♭ G B
C D E♭ F G A♭ B C	Fm	IV	F A♭ C
C D E♭ F G A♭ B C	G	V	G B D
C D E♭ F G A♭ B C	A♭	VI	A♭ C E♭
C D E♭ F G A♭ B C	B°	VII	B D F

All harmonic minor scales produce this pattern of triads.

Degree	I	II	III	IV	V	VI	VII
Type of triad	minor	diminished	augmented	minor	major	major	diminished

Notice that the triads on the 1st and 4th degrees are minor, the triads on the 2nd and 7th degrees are diminished, the triad on the 3rd degree is augmented and the triads on the 5th and 6th degrees are major.

Here is the C harmonic scale with the four note chords that can be built by using alternate notes on each degree of the scale.

C harmonic minor scale	chord symbol	degree	chord tones
C D E♭ F G A♭ B C	Cm/maj7	I	C E♭ G B
C D E♭ F G A♭ B C	Dm7♭5	II	D F A♭ C
C D E♭ F G A♭ B C	E♭maj7♯5	III	E♭ G B D
C D E♭ F G A♭ B C	Fm7	IV	F A♭ C E♭
C D E♭ F G A♭ B C	G7	V	G B D F
C D E♭ F G A♭ B C	A♭maj7	VI	A♭ C E♭ G
C D E♭ F G A♭ B C	B°7	VII	B D F A♭

All harmonic minor scales produce this pattern of chords.

Degree	I	II	III	IV	V	VI	VII
Type of chord	minor/major 7th	minor 7th♭5	major 7th♯5	minor 7th	dominant 7th	major 7th	diminished 7th

Notice that each degree of the scale produces a different chord type. Some of these chord types are the same as those built from major and natural minor scales. Here are how the additional chord types are constructed:

Minor/major 7th chords

- a flattened (minor) third interval between the root and the third
- a perfect fifth interval between the root and the fifth
- a major seventh interval between the root and the seventh

Major 7th ♯5 chords

- a major third interval between the root and the third
- a sharpened (augmented) fifth interval between the root and the fifth
- a major seventh interval between the root and the seventh

Diminished 7th chords

- a flattened (minor) third interval between the root and the third
- a flattened (diminished) fifth interval between the root and the fifth
- a double flattened (diminished) seventh interval between the root and the seventh

A double flattened seventh interval (also known as a diminished seventh interval) is one half step smaller than a flattened seventh (minor seventh) interval.

chord spellings

Each note in a chord is given a number, which refers to the interval between that note and the root of the chord. This is called the *chord spelling*. Each type of chord has a unique chord spelling and all chord types are numbered, and the intervals named, in comparison to the major scale. This enables easy comparison between different chord types.

The table below gives the chord spelling of the main chord types required for the Grade Six exam.

Major triads	1	3	5	
Minor triads	1	♭3	5	
Diminished triads	1	♭3	♭5	
Augmented triads	1	3	♯5	
sus 2 chords	1	2	5	
sus 4 chords	1	4	5	
5th 'power chords'	1	5	8	
Major 7th chords	1	3	5	7
Minor 7th chords	1	♭3	5	♭7
Dominant 7th chords	1	3	5	♭7
Minor 7th♭5 chords	1	♭3	♭5	♭7
Major 6th chords	1	3	5	6
Minor 6th chords	1	♭3	5	6
Major 9th chords	1	3	5	7	9
Minor 9th chords	1	♭3	5	♭7	9
Dominant 9th chords	1	3	5	♭7	9
Minor/major 7th chords	1	♭3	5	7
Major 7th♯5 chords	1	3	♯5	7
Diminished 7th chords	1	♭3	♭5	♭♭7

The chord spellings for inversions are simply re-arrangements of the original triad or chord – starting with whichever note has become the lowest in the inverted chord.

chord notation

Here are examples of each of the chord types that have been added for the Grade Six exam – all the other chord types have been covered in previous grades. You can work out the notes for other chord types, and chords with other root notes, by referring to the chord construction and chord spelling information given previously. Be careful to maintain the correct enharmonic spelling when notating chords by referring to the scale with the same starting note.

C diminished triad 1st inversion (C°/E♭)

Notice how the chord symbols are constructed for inversions: the basic chord symbol is written first, then a diagonal line followed by the lowest note.

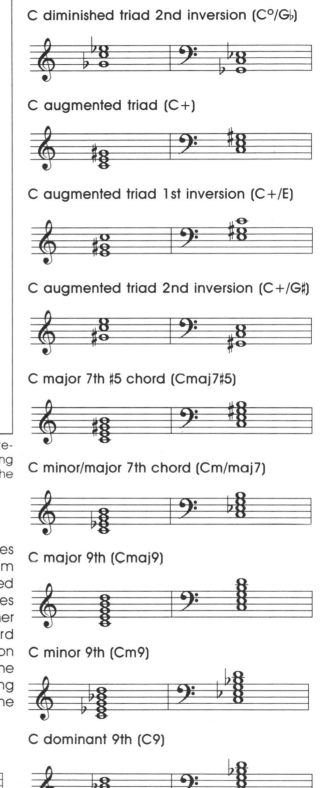

C diminished triad 2nd inversion (C°/G♭)

C augmented triad (C+)

C augmented triad 1st inversion (C+/E)

C augmented triad 2nd inversion (C+/G♯)

C major 7th ♯5 chord (Cmaj7♯5)

C minor/major 7th chord (Cm/maj7)

C major 9th (Cmaj9)

C minor 9th (Cm9)

C dominant 9th (C9)

As the requirements for each exam grade are cumulative it is essential that you thoroughly understand the requirements of the previous grades. It is particularly recommended that you revise the chord construction and chord spelling information given in the Grade Six section of this chapter before proceeding.

chord notation and spelling

Here are some examples of each of the chord types that have been added for the Grade Seven exam.

11th and 13th chords

Any dominant 7th or minor 7th chord can have an 11th chord extension added to it. The 11th will be the eleventh note of the *major* scale with the same keynote as the root of the chord. For example:

C major scale

C D E F G A B C D E F

1 2 3 4 5 6 7 8 9 10 11

C dominant 11th chord

C E G B♭ D F

1 3 5 ♭7 9 11

It is possible to add the 11th to major 7th chords, however, this chord is rarely used in popular music and so is not included in this book or series of exams.

Any major 7th, minor 7th or dominant 7th chord can have a 13th chord extension added to it. The 13th will be the thirteenth note of the *major* scale with the same keynote as the root of the chord. For example:

C major scale

C D E F G A B C D E F G A

1 2 3 4 5 6 7 8 9 10 11 12 13

C dominant 13th chord

C E G B♭ D F A

1 3 5 ♭7 9 11 13

C minor 11th (Cm11)

The chord spelling is: 1 ♭3 5 ♭7 9 11

C dominant 11th (C11)

The chord spelling is: 1 3 5 ♭7 9 11

C major 13th (Cmaj13)

The chord spelling is: 1 3 5 7 9 11 13

C minor 13th (Cm13)

The chord spelling is: 1 ♭3 5 ♭7 9 11 13

C dominant 13th (C13)

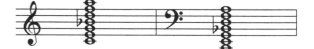

The chord spelling is: 1 3 5 ♭7 9 11 13

Chord voicing

For exam purposes, chords should be notated in 'close position' with all the notes placed in ascending order: starting with the root, then the 3rd, then the 5th etc. In practical playing, however, such rigidity is not necessary. Guitarists, for example, generally tend to *voice* chords (i.e. interchange the order of notes within a chord) according to the position of the chord on the guitar fingerboard and in relation to the chords which precede and follow it. In extended chords, all instrumentalists, tend to leave out certain notes in order to create a more defined sound: in 11th chords sometimes the 9th is omitted; in major 13th and dominant 13th chords the 11th is nearly always omitted in order to avoid dissonance with the 3rd of the chord.

C dominant 7th #5

This consists of:

■ a major third interval between the root and the third

■ a sharpened (augmented) fifth interval between the root and the fifth

■ a flattened (minor) seventh interval between the root and the seventh

The chord spelling is: 1 3 #5 ♭7

C7#5

C dominant 7th ♭5

This consists of:

■ a major third interval between the root and the third

■ a flattened (diminished) fifth interval between the root and the fifth

■ a flattened (minor) seventh interval between the root and the seventh

The chord spelling is: 1 3 ♭5 ♭7

C7♭5

C minor 7th #5

This consists of:

■ a minor third interval between the root and the third

■ a sharpened (augmented) fifth interval between the root and the fifth

■ a flattened (minor) seventh interval between the root and the seventh

The chord spelling is: 1 ♭3 #5 ♭7

Cm7#5

C minor 7th ♭5

This consists of:

■ a minor third interval between the root and the third

■ a flattened (diminished) fifth interval between the root and the fifth

■ a flattened (minor) seventh interval between the root and the seventh

The chord spelling is: 1 ♭3 ♭5 ♭7

Cm7♭5

chord inversions

1st, 2nd and 3rd inversions of major 7th, minor 7th and dominant 7th chords are created in a similar way to inversions of triads.

■ In 1st inversion the third becomes the lowest note.

■ In 2nd inversion the fifth becomes the lowest note.

■ In 3rd inversion the seventh becomes the lowest note.

Strictly speaking, chord inversions should maintain the progressive order of notes (as notated below). However, in popular music the term 'inversion' is widely used (particularly amongst guitarists) simply to refer to any chord in which a chord tone other than the root is placed as the lowest note in the chord.

Here are examples of major 7th, minor 7th and dominant 7th chords shown in 1st, 2nd and 3rd inversions.

C major 7th inversions

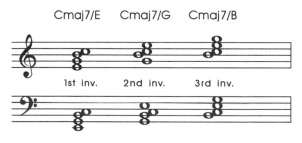

C minor 7th inversions

    Cm7/E♭   Cm7/G   Cm7/B♭

C dominant 7th inversions

    C7/E   C7/G   C7/B♭

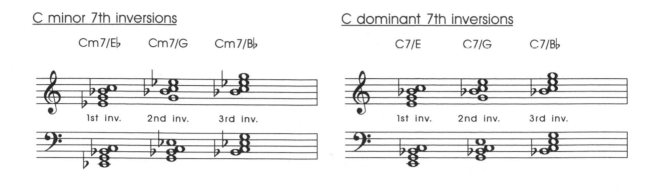

1st inv.   2nd inv.   3rd inv.   1st inv.   2nd inv.   3rd inv.

grade eight

As the requirements for each exam grade are cumulative it is essential that you thoroughly understand the requirements of the previous grades. It is particularly recommended that you revise the chord construction and chord spelling information given in the Grade Six and Seven sections of this chapter before proceeding.

Here are examples of each of the additional chord types that are required for the Grade Eight exam.

sharp and flat 9ths

A sharpened (augmented) 9th interval is one half step larger than a major 9th interval, and a flattened 9th interval is one half step smaller than a major 9th interval. For example, the note which is a major 9th interval above C is D. The note which is a sharpened 9th above C is therefore D♯, and the note which is a flattened 9th above C is D♭.

C dominant 7th ♯9 (C7♯9)

The chord spelling for dominant 7th ♯9 chords is: 1 3 5 ♭7 ♯9

C dominant 7th ♭9 (C7♭9)

The chord spelling for dominant 7th ♭9 chords is: 1 3 5 ♭7 ♭9

C minor 7th ♭9 (Cm7♭9)

The chord spelling for minor 7th ♭9 chords is: 1 ♭3 5 ♭7 ♭9

sharp 11ths

A sharpened 11th interval is one half step larger than a perfect 11th interval. A sharpened 11th, rather than a *natural* 11th, is often added to major 7th and dominant 7th chords. In popular music, the 9th note in ♯11th chords is normally omitted in practice. However, the chords are notated below in full.

C major 7th ♯11 (Cmaj7♯11)

The chord spelling for major 7th ♯11 chords is 1 3 5 7 9 ♯11

C dominant 7th ♯11 chord (C7♯11)

The chord spelling for dominant 7th ♯11 chords is 1 3 5 ♭7 9 ♯11

Altered bass 'slash chords'

'Slash chord' is the term commonly used to refer to a chord in which the lowest note is a note other than the root.

The chord symbol is written as normal but with a diagonal line (slash) after it and the bass note following the line. For example, if the C major chord is to be played with the note E in the bass it would be written as C/E. This method of specifying the bass note can be used to describe chord inversions, but it can also describe any chord type – including those in which the bass note does not appear in the original chord (i.e. where a chord has an *altered* bass note which is not a chord tone). For example, C/A is the C major triad with the note A in the bass.

Here are some examples of commonly used 'slash chords'.

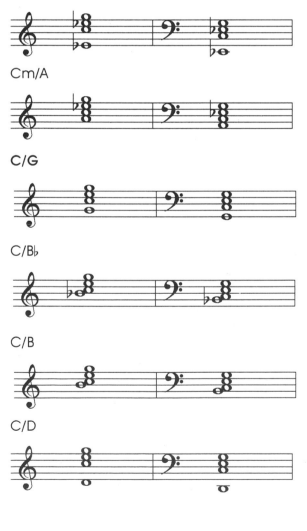

'Add chords'

'Add chord' is the term commonly used to refer to a chord in which an extension is added to a chord, without any intermediary notes being included. For example, Cadd9 means add the 9th (of the C major scale) to the C major triad. The notes would therefore be C E G D (1 3 5 9). So, in Cadd9 the 7th is *not* included, unlike Cmaj9 which does include the 7th.

Cadd9

The same principle applies to minor triads.

Cmadd9

There follows some examples of the types of questions that candidates may be asked at Grades Six, Seven and Eight in this section of the exam. All chords should be written in 'root position' unless stated otherwise. If you are unable to answer a question, then carefully re-read the preceding chapter. If necessary, refer to the preceding books in this series.

Sample questions for Grade Six

Q1.   Write out the A♭maj7♯5 chord in the treble clef.

A1.

Q2.   Write out the B9 chord in the bass clef.

A2.

Q3.   In the treble clef, write out the C augmented triad in 2nd inversion.

A3.

Q4.   Write out the Em9 chord in the bass clef.

A4.

Q5.   Write out the chord spelling of the following chords:

A5.   Major 9th: _____

Minor 9th: _____

Dominant 9th: _____

Sample questions for Grade Seven

Q1. In the treble clef, write out the D♯m11 chord.

A1.

Q2. In the treble clef, write out the D♭7♯5 chord.

A2.

Q3. In the bass clef, write out the Bmaj7 chord in 3rd inversion.

A3.

Q4. In the bass clef, write out the E13 chord.

A4.

Q5. Write out the chord spelling of the following chords:

A5. Dominant 11th: _____

Major 13th: _____

Minor 13th: _____

Sample questions for Grade Eight

Q1. In the treble clef, write out the Gmaj7#11 chord.

A1.

Q2. In the bass clef, write out the Fm/A♭ slash chord.

A2.

Q3. In the treble clef, write out the A♭add9 chord.

A3.

Q4. In the bass clef, write out the Dm7♭9 chord.

A4.

Q5. Write out the chord spelling of the following chords:

A5. Dominant 7th #9: _____

Minor 7th ♭9: _____

Dominant 7th #11: _____

Section Three – rhythm notation

In this section of the exam you should have a good practical understanding of:

- whole notes (semibreves)
- half notes (minims)
- quarter notes (crotchets)
- eighth notes (quavers)
- sixteenth notes (semiquavers)
- 32nd notes (demisemiquavers)
- 64th notes (hemidemisemiquavers)
- Dotted notes and dotted rests
- Tied notes
- Triplets

- whole rests (semibreve rests)
- half rests (minim rests)
- quarter rests (crotchet rests)
- eighth rests (quaver rests)
- sixteenth rests (semiquaver rests)
- 32nd rests (demisemiquaver rests)
- 64th rests (hemidemisemiquaver rests)

So that the rhythm notation learnt in theory can be used effectively in a practical way, you should be able to do the following:

- Group notes and rests correctly within the time signatures listed for each grade.
- Add bar lines to given rhythms.
- Compose rhythmic patterns using the note and rest values listed.

Rhythm notation requirements for Grade Six

- $\frac{2}{4}$ $\frac{3}{4}$ $\frac{4}{4}$ $\frac{6}{8}$ $\frac{9}{8}$ and $\frac{12}{8}$ time signatures
- syncopated rhythms

Rhythm notation requirements for Grade Seven

- As for Grade Six, but including $\frac{5}{4}$ time signatures and rhythms of greater complexity.

Rhythm notation requirements for Grade Eight

- As for Grade Seven, but including $\frac{3}{2}$ $\frac{3}{2}$ $\frac{6}{4}$ $\frac{7}{4}$ $\frac{3}{8}$ and $\frac{7}{8}$ time signatures and rhythms of greater complexity.

In this book we concentrate on the additional rhythm requirements that have been included at these advanced grades. If you have difficulty in understanding any of the concepts used it is recommended that you refer to the previous books in this series which fully cover the basics of rhythm notation, including information on: time signatures; rules concerning the grouping of notes and rests; use of dotted notes, tied notes and triplets.

grade six

time signatures

- $\frac{2}{4}$, $\frac{3}{4}$ and $\frac{4}{4}$ are all known as *simple time signatures*. In these time signatures each beat is represented by a quarter note and can be divided into two pulses.

- $\frac{6}{8}$, $\frac{9}{8}$ and $\frac{12}{8}$ are *compound time signatures*. In these time signatures each beat is represented by a dotted quarter note and can be divided into three pulses.

- Time signatures with two beats per bar are known as *duple time*: $\frac{2}{4}$ = simple duple time; $\frac{6}{8}$ = compound duple time.

- Time signatures with three beats per bar are known as *triple time*: $\frac{3}{4}$ = simple triple time; $\frac{9}{8}$ = compound triple time.

- Time signatures with four beats per bar are known as *quadruple time*: $\frac{4}{4}$ = simple quadruple time; $\frac{12}{8}$ = compound quadruple time.

32nd and 64th notes

- A 32nd note (demisemiquaver) lasts for half the length of a 16th note (semiquaver). The following example shows a combination of 16th and 32nd notes and rests:

- A 64th note (hemidemisemiquaver) lasts for half the length of a 32nd note. Therefore, four 64th notes can fit in the time of one 16th note. The following example shows a combination of 32nd and 64th notes and rests (ending with a quarter rest):

grade seven

As the requirements for each exam grade are cumulative it is essential that you thoroughly understand the requirements of the previous grades. It is particularly recommended that you revise the Grade Six section of this chapter before proceeding.

$\frac{5}{4}$ time

$\frac{5}{4}$ is a *quintuple* time signature, which has five quarter note beats in each bar. These can be grouped either as a group of three and a group of two (3+2), or as a group of two and a group of three (2+3). Either way, notes should be grouped to show the subdivisions of the bar.

Grouped as 3+2.

grouping of notes and rests

There are important general 'rules' about how notes and rests can be combined so that all beats of the bar can be clearly identified, and consequently the written music is easier to read. These principles are fully covered in the Grade Five handbook, which you should refer to if necessary. You will notice below that when syncopation is used, these general 'rules' are sometimes broken to avoid excessive notational complexity.

syncopation

Syncopation occurs when accents are moved from the strong beats of a bar to ones that are normally weak. The simplest way to achieve this is by placing rests on normally strong beats so that the weaker beats are emphasised. For example:

A short note followed by a long note also tends to give a syncopated effect.

Grouped as 2+3.

syncopation

As described at Grade Six, syncopation can be achieved by placing rests on normally strong beats so that weaker beats are emphasised. However, syncopation can also be achieved by holding over a note that first occurs on a weak beat to an accented position, or by placing an accent on a normally weak beat. For example:

As the requirements for each exam grade are cumulative it is essential that you thoroughly understand the requirements of the previous grades. It is particularly recommended that you revise the Grades Six and Seven sections of this chapter before proceeding.

time signatures

Here are the new time signatures that have been added for the Grade Eight exam:

Simple time signatures

- $\frac{3}{8}$ contains three eighth note beats per bar and is called a *simple triple* time signature

- $\frac{2}{2}$ contains two half note beats per bar and is called a *simple duple* time signature

- $\frac{3}{2}$ contains three half note beats per bar and is called a *simple triple* time signature

The rules for the grouping of notes and rests within these time signatures are the same as for all other simple time signatures (such as $\frac{3}{4}$ and $\frac{2}{4}$), but with the value of the beats halved (in $\frac{3}{8}$) or doubled (in $\frac{2}{2}$ and $\frac{3}{2}$). Notice that in $\frac{3}{8}$ time all 8th and 16th notes can be grouped together.

becomes

becomes

becomes

Compound time signatures

$\frac{6}{4}$ is a *compound duple* time signature: it contains two dotted half note beats (i.e. six quarter note pulses, arranged in two groups of three). The rules for the grouping of notes and rests within this time signature are the same as for the compound time signatures covered at earlier grades ($\frac{6}{8}$, $\frac{9}{8}$, $\frac{12}{8}$) but with the values of the notes and rests doubled.

For example:

becomes

In $\frac{6}{4}$ time, and in $\frac{3}{2}$ time, a dotted whole note can be used to fill a whole bar, as can a whole note rest.

Other time signatures

$\frac{7}{4}$ and $\frac{7}{8}$ are both *septuple* time signatures, as these both contain seven beats in each bar. These are usually grouped as 2 + 2 (or 4) + 3, or 3 + 2 + 2 (or 4). Either way, notes should be grouped to show the subdivisions of the bar.

Grouped as 2+2+3.

Grouped as 3+4.

syncopation

In addition to the methods outlined in previous grades, another effective way of achieving syncopation is by a change of time signature.

There follows some examples of the types of questions that candidates may be asked at Grades Six, Seven and Eight in this section of the exam. If you are unable to answer a question, then carefully re-read the preceding chapter. If necessary, refer to the preceding books in this series.

Sample questions for Grade Six

Q1.   Re-write the following two bars correctly.

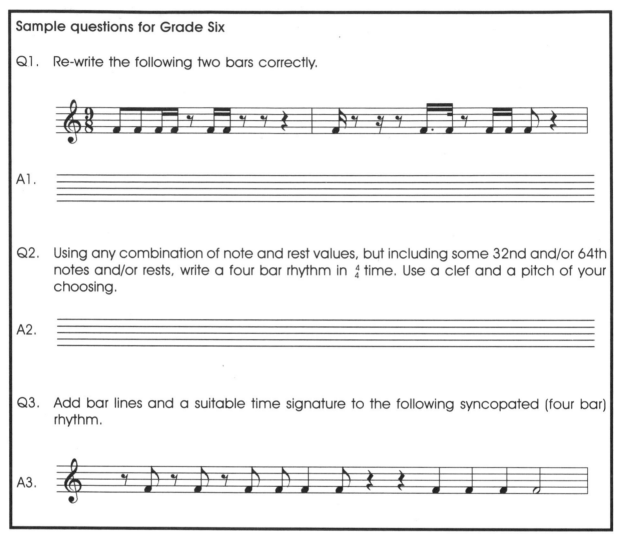

A1.

Q2.   Using any combination of note and rest values, but including some 32nd and/or 64th notes and/or rests, write a four bar rhythm in $\frac{4}{4}$ time. Use a clef and a pitch of your choosing.

A2.

Q3.   Add bar lines and a suitable time signature to the following syncopated (four bar) rhythm.

A3.

Sample questions for Grade Seven

Q1. Re-write the following two bars correctly.

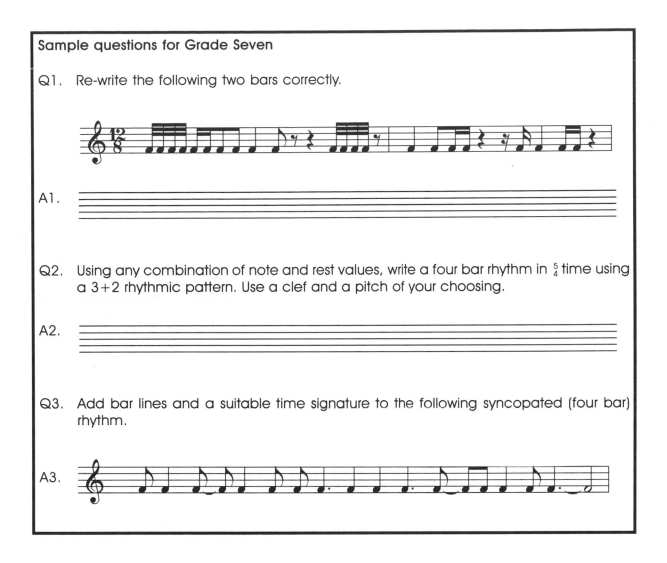

A1.

Q2. Using any combination of note and rest values, write a four bar rhythm in $\frac{5}{4}$ time using a 3+2 rhythmic pattern. Use a clef and a pitch of your choosing.

A2.

Q3. Add bar lines and a suitable time signature to the following syncopated (four bar) rhythm.

A3.

Sample questions for Grade Eight

Q1.   Re-write the following eight bars correctly.

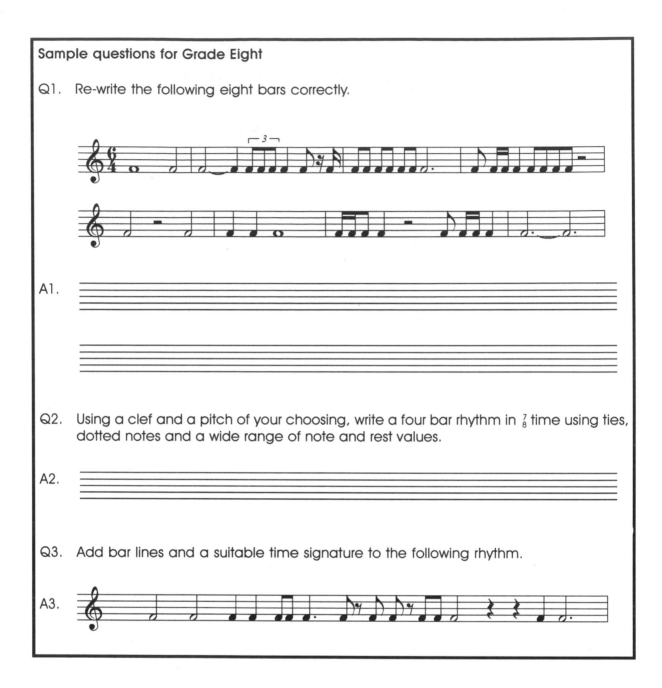

A1.

Q2.   Using a clef and a pitch of your choosing, write a four bar rhythm in $\frac{7}{8}$ time using ties, dotted notes and a wide range of note and rest values.

A2.

Q3.   Add bar lines and a suitable time signature to the following rhythm.

A3.

Section Four – popular music

In this section of the exam you will be asked to write an essay, of approximately 400 to 500 words, answering ONE of the questions given from a choice of two questions.

Popular music requirements for Grade Six

A good knowledge of the history of popular music from 1950, including an in-depth knowledge and understanding of popular music styles.

Popular music requirements for Grade Seven

As for Grade Six, but in greater depth, plus a wider knowledge of the history and development of popular music dating back before 1950, where necessary, and including the influence of technological developments.

Popular music requirements for Grade Eight

As for Grade Seven, but in greater depth, and with a wider knowledge of the history and development of popular music throughout the 20th century, including the influence of other forms of music and the societal contexts.

General guidance

On the following page are some examples of the types of questions you may be asked at each grade, and some guidance as to the type of information you are required to present. (The term 'musicians' in the context of this chapter includes: groups, instrumentalists, vocalists, composers and songwriters.)

You will need to carry out your own research in advance in order to fully prepare for this section of the exam. This may involve listening to recordings and reading biographies and encyclopaedias of popular music. The latter can be obtained from good libraries and bookshops, or from music education publishers and distributors (such as Registry Publications +44 (0)20 8665 7666), or via specialist internet suppliers (such as www.BooksForMusic.com).

As you will see from the sample questions, there are no 'set' musicians, so your success in this section of the exam will very much depend upon the amount of research and preparation you undertake.

Questions at Grade Six require a detailed knowledge of:

a) at least two different styles of popular music – so you should research the following information:

(i)   the main features of each style;

(ii)   the main exponents of each style;

(iii)   when each style was developed and played;

(iv)   how each style developed.

b) the career of at least two groups, vocalists or instrumentalists, (one of whom should have covered more than one musical style during their career); you should research the following information:

(i)   dates of the musicians' careers, including when different styles were played;

(ii)   the main features of any styles played;

(iii)   how each style developed;

(iv)   how the musicians contributed to the development of a style.

Sample questions

Q1.   Choose a style of popular music and, with reference to at least two of this style's most well-known musicians, describe the main features of the musical style and outline its development.

Q2.   Choose two different styles of music and compare and contrast the differences between the main features of each style of music.

Q3.   Choose a group, vocalist or instrumentalist known for more than one style of music during their career and describe how the development of each style occurred, mentioning each style's main features.

Q4.   Choose two groups, vocalists, or instrumentalists who have both been involved in the same style of music, and describe how both have contributed to the development of that style.

Questions at Grade Seven require a detailed knowledge of:

a) at least two different styles of popular music – so you should research the following information:

(i)   the main features of each style;

(ii) the main exponents of each style;

(iii) when each style was developed and played;

(iv) how each style developed;

(v)   how each style has been influenced by musicians who were active before 1950;

(vi) how each style has been affected by technical innovations (such as recording techniques and instrument development);

b) the careers of at least two groups, vocalists or instrumentalists (one should be well known for more than one style of music); you should research the following information:

(i)   dates of the musicians' careers;

(ii) the main features of any musical styles played;

(iii) how the styles developed;

(iv) how the styles have been influenced by musicians who were active before 1950;

(v)   how technical innovations have influenced the styles of music;

(vi) how the musicians contributed to the development of a style of music.

Sample Questions

Q1.   Discuss, with reference to at least two well-known groups, instrumentalists or vocalists, how one or more technical innovations have influenced a particular style of music and how this has changed the course of popular music.

Q2.   Choose one successful group, vocalist, instrumentalist or songwriter and explain how that group's or individual's musical style has been influenced by musicians from an earlier period (including pre-1950 where appropriate).

Q3.   Discuss, with reference to at least two well-known post-1950 groups, instrumentalists, vocalists or songwriters, how musicians active before 1950 have influenced a particular style of music and how this has changed the course of popular music.

Q4.   Choose one successful group, vocalist or instrumentalist and describe how that group's or individual's music has evolved during their career. Explain how developments in musical technology and recording techniques have affected their music.

Questions at Grade Eight require a detailed knowledge of:

a) at least two different styles of popular music, so you should research the following information:

(i)   the main features of each style;

(ii)   the main exponents of each style;

(iii)   when each style was developed and played;

(iv)   how each style developed;

(v)   how the styles have been influenced by musicians who were active before 1950;

(vi)   how the styles have been influenced by technical innovations;

(vii)   how the styles have been influenced by the societal context;

(viii) how the styles have been influenced by other forms of music.

b) the careers of at least three groups, vocalists or instrumentalists (one should be well-known for more than one style of music); you should research the following information:

(i)   dates of the musicians' careers;

(ii)   the main features of any musical styles played;

(iii)   how the styles developed;

(iv)   how the styles have been influenced by musicians who were active before 1950;

(v)   how technical innovations have influenced the styles of music;

(vi)   how the musicians contributed to the development of a style of music;

(vii)   how their musical styles have been influenced by the societal context;

(viii) how their musical styles have been influenced by other forms of music.

Sample Questions

Q1.   Describe, with reference to at least three well-known groups, instrumentalists, vocalists or songwriters, how a post-1950 style of popular music has been influenced by musicians active before 1950.

Q2.   Choose a style of popular music, and with reference to at least three well-known groups, instrumentalists, vocalists or songwriters describe how the societal context influenced the way in which the music developed.

Q3.   Choose a successful group, instrumentalist, vocalist or songwriter and describe how that group's or individual's music has been influenced by another form of music – outlining the main features of both types of music.

Q4.   Choose a successful group, instrumentalist, vocalist or songwriter and describe how that group's or individual's music has been influenced by the societal context in which their career developed; include information on the main features of their music.

Section Five – harmony

In this section of each exam you will be asked to apply your knowledge of the scales and chords from Section One and Two to improvisation and to constructing and identifying chord progressions and cadential movements.

Harmony requirements for Grade Six

In a range of keys up to and including 5 sharps and 5 flats:

- the patterns of major 7th, minor 7th, dominant 7th and minor 7th ♭5 chords built from major and natural minor scales;

- constructing and identifying commonly occurring cadential chord movements;

- constructing and analysing chord progressions using chords built from major and natural minor scales, the dominant 7th chord built from the harmonic minor scale and chords built from the following:
  Dorian modal scales – D, A, E, B, F♯, C♯, G, C, F, B♭ and E♭.
  Mixolydian modal scales – G, D, A, E, B, F♯, C, F, B♭, E♭ and A♭
  Lydian modal scales – F, C, G, D, A, E, B♭, E♭, A♭, D♭ and G♭

- the application of scales and modal scales from Section 1 in improvisation.

Harmony requirements for Grade Seven

In ALL keys:

- the patterns of major 7th, minor 7th, dominant 7th and minor 7th ♭5 chords built from major and natural minor scales;

- constructing and identifying commonly occurring cadential chord movements;

- constructing and analysing chord progressions using: chords built from major and natural minor scales; the dominant 7th chord built from the harmonic minor scale; chords built from Dorian, Lydian, Mixolydian and Phrygian modal scales;

- constructing and analysing chord progressions involving key changes to near and related keys;

- using chord symbols to harmonise a melody in any key;

- the application of scales and modal scales from Section 1 in improvisation, including recognition of key changes to near and related keys.

Harmony requirements for Grade Eight

In ALL keys:

- all the requirements set for Grade seven, plus:

- constructing and analysing chord progressions involving modulation to any key;

- analysing chord progressions which use non-diatonic chords;

- using chord symbols to harmonise a melody that may modulate to any near or related key;

- the application of scales and modal scales from Section 1 in improvisation, including recognition of modulations to any key.

In this book we will explain the theory behind the additional harmony that you are required to know for each grade and summarise the harmony that has been covered in the previous books in this series. If you are unsure of any of the terms or concepts used, you are advised to refer to the earlier books in this series.

the theory

The type of chord that can be built, by taking alternate notes, from each degree of a major scale is always the same for each particular scale degree, regardless of the key.

All major keys have the following pattern of chords:

I	II	III	IV	V	VI	VII
major 7th	minor 7th	minor 7th	major 7th	dominant 7th	minor 7th	minor 7th ♭5

Notice that the chords built on the 1st and 4th degrees are major 7th chords, the chords built on the 2nd, 3rd and 6th degrees are minor 7th chords, the chord built on the 5th degree is a dominant 7th chord and the chord built on the 7th degree is a minor 7th ♭5 chord.

The type of chord that can be built, by taking alternate notes, from each degree of a natural minor scale is always the same for each particular scale degree, regardless of the key.

All natural minor keys have the following pattern of chords:

I	II	III	IV	V	VI	VII
minor 7th	minor 7th ♭5	major 7th	minor 7th	minor 7th	major 7th	dominant 7th

Notice that the chords built on the 1st, 4th and 5th degrees are all minor 7th chords, the chords built on the 3rd and 6th degrees are major 7th chords, the chord built on the 7th degree is a dominant 7th chord and the chord built on the 2nd degree is a minor 7th ♭5 chord.

Degrees of the scale and the chords which are built on them, are traditionally, and still widely, identified using Roman numerals. This system is very useful as it provides a straightforward method of identifying the type of chord as well as the position of the chord in the scale. Here are the major 7th, minor 7th, dominant 7th and minor 7th ♭5 chords in the key of C major and A natural minor identified using this system. (In the exam, candidates are free to use the 'Nashville numbering system' if preferred).

C major	Chord:	Cmaj7	Dm7	Em7	Fmaj7	G7	Am7	Bm7♭5
	Roman numerals:	Imaj7	IIm7	IIIm7	IVmaj7	V7	VIm7	VIIm7♭5

A natural minor	Chord:	Am7	Bm7♭5	Cmaj7	Dm7	Em7	Fmaj7	G7
	Roman numerals:	Im7	IIm7♭5	♭IIImaj7	IVm7	Vm7	♭VImaj7	♭VII7

By using these two formulae you can find out which major 7th, minor 7th, dominant 7th and minor 7th ♭5 chords are formed from any major or natural minor scale.

Supplementary explanation

The chords built from the natural minor scale are numbered in comparison to the chords from the major scale with the same keynote. The flat sign before the chords built on the third, sixth and seventh degrees show that the roots of these chords are a half step (semitone) lower than the roots of the corresponding chords in the major scale with the same keynote.

For example, in the key of B major the third, sixth and seventh notes are D#, G# and A#, whereas in the scale of B natural minor the third, sixth and seventh notes are D, G and A. Therefore the roots of the chords built on these degrees of the natural minor scale are all a half step lower than the roots of the chords built on these degrees of the major scale and so a flat sign is inserted before the interval number to reflect this.

<u>dominant 7th chords from the harmonic minor</u>

The chord that is built, by taking four alternate notes, on the fifth degree of the harmonic minor is always a dominant seventh chord.

For example:

A harmonic minor	E dominant 7th
A <u>B</u> C <u>D</u> *E* F G# A	E G# B D

G# harmonic minor	D# dominant 7th
G# A#̸ B C#̸ *D#̸* E F×̸ G#	D# F× A#̸ C#̸

B♭ harmonic minor	F dominant 7th
B♭ <u>C</u> D♭ <u>E♭</u> *F* G♭ <u>A</u> B♭	F A C E♭

In order to create a stronger resolution, the V – I cadence in a chord progression based on the natural minor scale often 'borrows' the fifth chord of the harmonic minor scale. The fifth chord of the harmonic minor scale is a dominant 7th chord which creates a very strong sense of release when it resolves to the I chord.

<u>building chords from modal scales</u>

Chords can be built, by taking alternate notes, from each degree of a modal scale in the same way that they can be built from major and natural minor scales. The pattern that occurs in each modal scale will be explained more fully under the requirements for each grade.

constructing chord progressions

In popular music there are no 'rules' about which chords should be used at particular points in a piece of music, however there are some combinations of chords which are often used to create *cadential movements* in order to give the music structure and shape.

The most common cadences, V – I (perfect) and IV – I (plagal), have been thoroughly explained in earlier books in this series. Here are some of the other most common cadential movements:

- The V chord is often used as a temporary resting place during a piece of music, for example at the end of a verse before a chorus. In this cadence (which is traditionally known as the *imperfect cadence*) the V chord is usually approached by the I chord: in C major the cadence would be C to G, or C to G7.

- The V chord is often followed by a chord other than the I chord. For example, the V chord is sometimes followed by the VI chord. (This is traditionally known as an *interrupted cadence*). In C major this chord movement could be G to Em.

- In keys based on the natural minor scale, the ♭VI or ♭VII chords are often used to lead back to the I chord – as both these movements create a sense of resolution. For example, in A minor: F to Am (♭VI to I); G to Am (♭VII to I).

The most important factor regarding all of the above examples is how effective they sound in any particular piece of music. We recommend that, if possible, you play them on your instrument and experiment with them and other chord combinations when you are practising writing songs or chord progressions.

Below are a few tips on writing chord progressions in major and minor keys that may be helpful:

- So that you can choose from the full range of chords, you need to know all the common chords that are in the key. You can work them out by using the formulae given previously.

- Starting the chord progression with the *key chord* will help to instantly define the pitch and tonality of the key.

- Using a V – I or IV – I cadence (in major keys and minor keys based on the natural minor scale) or a ♭VII – I cadence (in a minor key based on the natural minor scale) at the end of the progression will help to create a sense of 'reaching a resting point' or a feeling of 'arriving home'.

- Using the V chord from the harmonic minor scale in minor keys will similarly help to create a sense of 'arriving home' once it resolves to the I chord.

- V – I and V – VI cadences can be used in both major and minor keys to provide structure and shape to a progression.

Although many chord progressions use cadences to indicate the end of a musical phrase, it is not essential that phrases end in this way. When writing chord progressions, the most important consideration is *do the chords you have used create the musical effect you intended?*

using chord extensions and variations

Using a chord extension does not fundamentally change the function of a chord, consequently chord extensions are often used as a straightforward way of making a chord progression sound more interesting. (For example, the I and IV chords in a major key can be extended to become Imaj9 and IVmaj9). Chord extensions are also used to match or contrast with notes in a melody line or riff. Careful use of chord extensions can also enable a smoother transition to the next chord in a progression. We recommend that you experiment with a wide range of chord extensions when practising writing chord progressions.

In order to achieve a wide variety of musical sounds when composing chord progressions, you should also consider using other chords that you have learnt at lower grades, such as major and minor triads, inversions, 'sus chords', 5th 'power chords', major 6th and minor 6th chords. The use of all these chord types has been explained in previous grades.

writing blues-based chord progressions

The harmony used in blues-based music falls outside standard musical harmony. The chords in blues-based music are normally dominant 7ths (i.e. extensions of *major* triads), but melodies and improvisations are often based on the blues scale which can be viewed as a variation of the pentatonic *minor* scale. It is the unique clash and dissonance between these two key types that gives blues music its distinctive sound.

There are no 'rules' in writing blues-based chord progressions, but the chords that are often used are the dominant 7th chords built on the 1st, 4th and 5th degrees of the scale, although a variety of other chords can occur according to different stylistic traditions. For example, in a blues-based chord progression in C, the chords that are often used are C7, F7 and G7. However, A♭, B♭ and E♭ triads also commonly occur and, if the music is stylistically in the rock tradition, 5th 'power chords' are often used.

chord progressions using modal harmony

There are no strict 'rules' in writing chord progressions using modal harmony – the most important factor is whether the combination of chords create the effect that you intend. However, there are some methods that can be used to construct chord progressions that best reflect the sound of a particular modal scale. These will be explained more fully in the requirements for each grade that follow later in this chapter.

improvisation

Major and pentatonic major scales are used for improvising in major keys. For example, if a chord progression uses chords from the key of E major, then the E major or E major pentatonic scale would be an appropriate scale to use for improvising.

Natural minor and pentatonic minor scales are used for improvising in minor keys. For example, if a chord progression uses chords from the key of C♯ minor, then the C♯ natural minor or C♯ pentatonic minor scale would normally be an appropriate scale to use for improvising.

Blues scales are the main scales used for improvising over blues-based chord progressions. The chords used to accompany this scale are normally dominant 7th chords, although other chords types can also be used.

Modal scales are used for improvising over chord progressions written using modal harmony. Some of these progressions may be essentially 'major' or 'minor', however the particular combination of chords will dictate which modal scale should be used. This will be explained more fully in the requirements for each grade that follow later in this chapter.

chord analysis and scale choices

The most reliable method of deciding which scale to use over a chord progression is to first analyse the chords to assess the key to which they belong.

The chords built from any major scale and its relative (natural) minor are the same, and it is therefore important to look at how the chord progression is structured in order to identify the key correctly. Normally, a chord progression will start and finish on the I (key) chord, and this will indicate whether the progression is in the major or relative minor key.

If the I chord in a key is a dominant 7th chord the music is likely to be blues-based, especially if the chords on the 4th and 5th degrees are also dominant 7th chords and there are other non-diatonic chords in the progression. For example, C blues scale would fit over any combination of C7, F7, G7, A♭, B♭ & E♭.

Once the key has been established the remainder of the chords can then be identified using the Roman Numeral numbering system and the appropriate scale choice can then be made.

Here are examples of chord progressions in major, minor and blues keys, identified using the Roman Numeral numbering system and with an appropriate scale choice indicated.

Sample chord progression in E major:

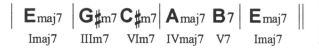

The E major scale or the E pentatonic major scale would be good scale choices for improvisation.

Sample chord progression in C♯ minor:

The C♯ natural minor scale or the C♯ pentatonic minor scale would be good scale choices for improvisation.

Sample chord progression for C blues scale:

| **C**7 | | **F**7 | | **A**♭ | **G**7 | **C**7 | |
| I7 | | IV7 | | ♭VI | V7 | I7 | |

The C blues scale would be a good scale choice for improvisation.

Further information about chord analysis and scale choices for chord progressions using modal harmony will be given in the requirements for each grade that follow later in this chapter.

When you are writing a chord progression to be used as a backing for improvisation the same process as described above applies. For major and minor keys work out the possible chords that can built on each degree of that scale, and then experiment with different possible combinations until you come up with some progressions that you like. Remember that using a V-I or IV-I cadence (in major and minor keys) or a ♭VII-I cadence (in minor keys) is a straightforward and effective way to create an ending to a progression.

For blues-based progressions work out the dominant 7th chords which are built on the 1st, 4th and 5th degrees. For other chord options an investigation into different stylistic traditions is necessary as there are no given 'rules'.

For modal progressions it is best to emphasize the key chord in order to establish the tonality of the key.

For the Grade Six exam, as well as constructing chord progressions using major and natural minor harmony, you are also required to construct chord progressions using Dorian, Lydian and Mixolydian harmony. You must also be able to apply Dorian, Lydian and Mixolydian modal scales in improvisation. Each modal scale has a key centre and tonality in its own right (with its own group of chords), just as the major and natural minor scales do. In fact, both these scales are modal scales themselves – the major scale is also known as the *Ionian* modal scale and the natural minor scale is also known as the *Aeolian* modal scale. In classical music notation, modes, other than the Ionian (major scale), have not been considered as 'keys' in their own right. However, in popular music, modes often function as distinct keys. Consequently, within this book, in order to aid clarity, we will identify modal harmony by referring to the relevant modal 'keys' as individual entities.

Dorian harmony

Dorian keys are minor keys that contain the same chords as major keys, but with the chord formula starting on what was the II chord in the major key, so the pattern of chords in Dorian keys is as follows:

minor 7th	minor 7th	major 7th	dominant 7th	minor 7th	minor 7th♭5	major 7th

Here are some examples of Dorian modal scales, together with their numbering using the Roman Numeral system:

Roman Numerals:	Im7	IIm7	♭IIImaj7	IV7	Vm7	VIm7♭5	♭VIImaj7
D Dorian modal scale:	Dm7	Em7	Fmaj7	G7	Am7	Bm7♭5	Cmaj7
C♯ Dorian modal scale:	C♯m7	D♯m7	Emaj7	F♯7	G♯m7	A♯m7♭5	Bmaj7
E♭ Dorian modal scale:	E♭m7	Fm7	G♭maj7	A♭7	B♭m7	Cm7♭5	D♭maj7

By using this formula you can find out which major 7th, minor 7th, dominant 7th and minor 7th♭5 chords are formed from any Dorian modal scale.

Note that the chords in the Dorian modal scale are numbered in comparison to the chords in the major scale with the same keynote. The flat sign before the chords built on the third and seventh degrees show that the roots of these chords are a half step (semitone) lower than the roots of the corresponding chords from the major scale with the same keynote.

Chord progressions using Dorian harmony

There are no strict 'rules' for constructing chord progressions using Dorian harmony, but creating a Dorian chord progression is best achieved by using a combination of chords that most clearly define the particular sound of the Dorian modal scale. If the Im7 chord is used at the start this establishes both the key centre and the minor tonality. The Dorian modal scale and the natural minor scale, however, are both minor keys and have the same minor 7th key chord, so this alone will not establish that the key is Dorian. The note that distinguishes Dorian harmony from natural minor harmony is the sixth degree of the scale; the Dorian modal scale has a major 6th whilst the natural minor scale has a flattened 6th. Using triads or chords that contain this note will therefore establish whether the harmony is from the Dorian modal scale or the natural minor scale.

For example, here are the two scales starting from a D keynote:

D Dorian modal scale:	D E F G A B C D
D natural minor scale:	D E F G A B♭ C D

The sixth note is the only note that is different between the two scales.

Here are the two scales with the chords that can be built on each degree:

D Dorian modal scale:	Dm7	Em7	Fmaj7	G7	Am7	Bm7♭5	Cmaj7
D natural minor scale:	Dm7	Em7♭5	Fmaj7	Gm7	Am7	B♭maj7	C7

The Em7 and Bm7♭5 chords both contain the note B and would therefore be good chord choices for establishing the Dorian tonality of the key. The G7 also contains the note B, however care should be taken when using this chord to ensure that the effect of a V – I cadence in C major (G7-C) isn't created. This can be avoided by writing the G7 chord as a triad (i.e. without the seventh note) or by following it with a chord other than C. Other chords belonging to the D Dorian modal scale can also be used and you should experiment to find some combinations that you like.

Here are two examples of Dorian chord progressions to help you get started.

| **D**m7 | **E**m7 | **G**7 | **D**m ‖

| **D**m7 | **B**m7♭5 | **A**m7 **G** | **D**m7 ‖

Improvisation using the Dorian modal scale

The most reliable method of deciding which scale to use over a chord progression is to first analyse the chords to assess which key they stem from. Begin by assuming that the first chord is the key centre. If the chord is minor then the Dorian modal scale may be a possible scale choice, however other minor scales may also be possible scale choices. The remainder of the chords need to be analysed in order to establish which is the correct scale.

For example:

| Dm7 | Em7 | Dm7 | G7 ‖
Im7   IIm7   Im7   IV7

Analysis:

i. The progression starts with Dm7, thus implying a minor key and narrowing the scale choice down to either the D natural minor, D pentatonic minor scale or the D Dorian modal scale. (Other minor scale possibilities do exist, but these are the only minor scales you are required to know for the Grade Six exam.)

ii. The next chord, Em7, occurs only in D Dorian. D natural minor contains a B♭ note – whereas both the D Dorian modal scale and the Em7 chord contain a B natural.

iii. The appearance of G7 at the end of the progression confirms D Dorian modal scale as the best choice, as this chord can be built from the D Dorian modal scale, but not from the D natural minor scale.

Lydian Harmony

Lydian keys are major keys which contain the same chords as major keys, but with the chord formula starting on what was the IV chord in the major key, so the pattern of chords in Lydian keys is as follows:

major 7th	dominant 7th	minor 7th	minor 7th ♭5	major 7th	minor 7th	minor 7th

Here are some examples of Lydian modal scales, the chords that can be built from them and the Roman Numeral numbering system that can be used to describe them.

Roman Numerals:	Imaj7	II7	IIIm7	♯IVm7♭5	Vmaj7	VIm7	VIIm7
F Lydian modal scale:	Fmaj7	G7	Am7	Bm7♭5	Cmaj7	Dm7	Em7
E Lydian modal scale:	Emaj7	F♯7	G♯m7	A♯m7♭5	Bmaj7	C♯m7	D♯m7
G♭ Lydian modal scale:	G♭maj7	A♭7	B♭m7	Cm7♭5	D♭maj7	E♭m7	Fm7

By using this formula you can find out which major 7th, minor 7th, dominant 7th and minor 7th ♭5 chords are formed from any Lydian modal scale.

Note that the chords in the Lydian modal scale are numbered in comparison to the chords in the major scale with the same keynote. The sharp sign before the chord built on the fourth degree shows that the root of this chord is a half step (semitone) higher than the root of the corresponding chord from the major scale with the same keynote.

Chord progressions using Lydian harmony

There are no strict 'rules' for constructing chord sequences using Lydian harmony, but creating a Lydian chord progression is best achieved by using a combination of chords that most clearly define the particular sound of the Lydian modal scale. If the I chord is used, this establishes both the key centre and the major tonality. However, both the Lydian modal scale and the major scale are major keys and have the same major 7th key chord – so this alone will not establish that the key is Lydian. The note that distinguishes Lydian harmony from standard major key harmony is the fourth degree of the scale: the Lydian modal scale has a sharpened (augmented) 4th, whilst the major scale has a perfect 4th. Using chords that contain this note will therefore establish whether the harmony is from the Lydian modal scale or the major scale.

For example, here are the two scales starting from an F key note:

F Lydian modal scale:	F G A B C D E F
F major scale:	F G A B♭ C D E F

The fourth note is the only note that is different between the two scales.

Here are the two scales with the chords that can be built on each degree:

F Lydian modal scale:	Fmaj7	G7	Am7	Bm7♭5	Cmaj7	Dm7	Em7
F major scale:	Fmaj7	Gm7	Am7	B♭maj7	C7	Dm7	Em7♭5

The Em7 and Bm7♭5 chords both contain the note B and would therefore be good chord choices in helping establish a Lydian key centre. The G7 also contains the note B, however care should be taken when using this chord to ensure that the effect of a V – I cadence in C major (G7-C) isn't created. This can be avoided by writing the G7 chord as a triad (i.e. without the seventh note) or by following it with a chord other than C. Other chords belonging to the F Lydian modal scale can also be used and you should experiment to find some combinations that you like.

Here are two examples of Lydian chord progressions to help you get started.

| **F**maj7 | **G**7 | **D**m7 **E**m7 | **F**maj7 ‖

| **F**maj7 | **B**m7♭5 | **D**m7 | **E**m7 ‖

Improvisation using the Lydian modal scale

First analyse the chords in the progression to assess which key they stem from; begin by assuming that the first chord is the key centre. If the chord is a major 7th then the Lydian modal scale may be a possible scale choice. However, the major and pentatonic major scales may also be possible scale choices: in order to establish which is the correct scale, the remainder of the chords need to be analysed.

For example:

| Fmaj7 | Dm7 | Em7 | G7 ‖
| Imaj7 | VIm7 | VIIm7 | II7 |

Analysis:

i.   The progression starts with Fmaj7, thus implying a major key and narrowing the scale choice down to either the F major scale/F pentatonic major scale or the F Lydian modal scale.

ii. The next chord, Dm7, occurs in both F major and F Lydian – so this leaves us no further forward in identifying the overall key of the progression.

iii. The Em7 and G7 chords in the progression mean that the F Lydian modal scale would be the best choice, as both these chords occur in the key of F Lydian, whilst neither occur in the key of F major (which contains Em7b5 and Gm7 instead). The crucial difference is the B note (rather than F major's Bb) that occurs in the F Lydian modal scale and in both Em7 and G7.

Mixolydian Harmony

Mixolydian keys are dominant keys which contain the same chords as major keys, but with the chord formula starting on what was the V chord in the major key, so the pattern of chords in Mixolydian keys is as follows:

dominant 7th   minor 7th   minor 7th b5   major 7th   minor 7th   minor 7th   major 7th

Here are some examples of Mixolydian modal scales, the chords that can be built from them and the Roman Numeral numbering system that can be used to describe them.

Roman Numerals:	I7	IIm7	IIIm7b5	IVmaj7	Vm7	VIm7	bVIImaj7
G Mixolydian modal scale:	G7	Am7	Bm7b5	Cmaj7	Dm7	Em7	Fmaj7
F# Mixolydian modal scale:	F#7	G#m7	A#m7b5	Bmaj7	C#m7	D#m7	Emaj7
Ab Mixolydian modal scale:	Ab7	Bbm7	Cm7b5	Dbmaj7	Ebm7	Fm7	Gbmaj7

By using this formula you can find out which major 7th, minor 7th, dominant 7th and minor 7thb5 chords are formed from any Mixolydian modal scale.

Note that the chords in the Mixolydian modal scale are numbered in comparison to the chords in the major scale with the same keynote. The flat sign before the chord built on the seventh degree shows that the root of this chord is a half step (semitone) lower than the root of the corresponding chord in the major scale with the same keynote.

Chord progressions using Mixolydian harmony

There are no strict 'rules' for constructing chord progressions using Mixolydian harmony, but creating a Mixolydian chord progression is best achieved by using a combination of chords that most clearly define the particular sound of the Mixolydian modal scale. The I7 needs to be used in order to establish the sound of the Mixolydian modal scale. This is because the chord uses the flattened 7th note of the scale, which immediately distinguishes it from the major scale.

Here are the notes of the G Mixolydian modal scale and the G major scale starting from a G keynote:

G Mixolydian modal scale:	G A B C D E F G
G major scale:	G A B C D E F# G

The only note that is different between the two scales is the seventh – Fμ in G Mixolydian and F# in G major.

The other type of harmony which uses a dominant 7th chord as the key chord is blues-based music. However, in blues-based music, the IV and V chords are also dominant 7th chords, whereas in Mixolydian harmony the IV is a major 7th chord and the V chord is a minor 7th chord.

Here are the G Mixolydian modal scale and the G major scale with the chords that can be built on each degree:

G Mixolydian modal scale:	G7	Am7	Bm7♭5	Cmaj7	Dm7	Em7	Fmaj7
G major scale:	Gmaj7	Am7	Bm7	Cmaj7	D7	Em	F#m7♭5

As well as G7, other chords which contain F♮ such as Fmaj7, Dm7 and Bm7♭5 are all good chord choices in helping to establish the Mixolydian tonality. The remaining chords belonging to the G Mixolydian modal scale can also be used and you should experiment to find some combinations that you like.

Here are two examples of Mixolydian chord progressions to help you get started.

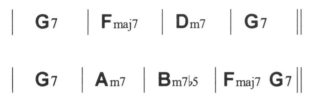

Improvisation using the Mixolydian modal scale

First analyse the chords in the progression to assess which key they stem from; begin by assuming that the first chord is the key chord. If this chord is a dominant 7th then the Mixolydian modal scale may be a suitable scale choice, however the blues scale may also be a possible scale choice. The remainder of the chords need to be analysed in order to establish which is the correct scale.

For example:

G7	Dm7	G7	Fmaj9 ‖
I7	Vm7	I7	♭VIImaj9

Analysis:

i. The progression starts with G7, thus implying a dominant key centre and narrowing the scale choice down to either the G blues or G Mixolydian modal scale.

ii. The next chord, Dm7, occurs in the key of G Mixolydian and not in the key of G blues, suggesting that the G Mixolydian modal scale would be the best scale choice.

iii. The final chord, Fmaj9, is merely an extension of Fmaj7 and so does not alter our scale choice of the G Mixolydian modal scale.

Improvisation using the harmonic minor and chromatic scales

These two scales are not used for improvising in the same way as the scales and modal scales described above. The scales discussed so far generate their own chords and are primarily used over chord progressions that use the relevant harmony.

Harmonic minor scales

The harmonic minor scale does generate its own chords (as described in Section Two), however, in popular music, chord progressions which use chords generated solely from the harmonic minor scale are very rare. More often, elements of the harmonic minor scale are used to give a tune or an improvisation a particular 'flavour'. For example, if a tune is in a minor key and only uses chords Im and V, then the harmonic minor scale would be a good alternative to the natural or pentatonic minor scales. This works particularly well if the music has a *Latin* feel. Another instance for using this scale (in higher grades) is over a minor/major 7th chord – as this is the key chord of the harmonic minor scale. We recommend that you experiment using the scale in a range of musical situations.

The chromatic scale

The chromatic scale can be used to generate chords, however this method of creating harmony is rare in popular music. Some of the most common uses of the chromatic scale in improvisation are to link phrases, or notes within a phrase, by using part of the scale as *passing notes*. For example, in the key of C, a phrase ending on a C note could be linked to a phrase starting on an A note by using part of the the chromatic scale – C B B♭ A. Using the scale in this way introduces non-diatonic notes and can add interest and colour to an improvisation. As with the harmonic minor scale, we recommend that you experiment with the scale in a range of musical situations.

The theory related to constructing chord progressions using major, natural minor, Dorian, Lydian and Mixolydian harmony and using these and the harmonic minor and chromatic scales for improvising has been covered in the previous sections in this book. For the Grade Seven exam you are required to apply this knowledge in the full range of keys. You are also required to:

- construct chord progressions using Phrygian harmony;

- construct chord progressions that change to near and related keys;

- identify scales from Section One that could be used for improvising over a given chord progression that may modulate to a near or related key;

- use chord symbols to harmonise a melody in any key.

Phrygian Harmony

Phrygian keys are minor keys which contain the same chords as major keys, but with the chord formula starting on what was the III chord in the major key, so the pattern of chords in Phrygian keys is as follows:

minor 7th	major 7th	dominant 7th	minor 7th	minor 7th $\flat$5	major 7th	minor 7th

Here are some examples of Phrygian keys, the chords that can be built from them and the Roman Numeral numbering system that can be used to describe them.

Roman Numerals:	Im7	$\flat$IImaj7	$\flat$III7	IVm7	Vm7$\flat$5	$\flat$VImaj7	$\flat$VIIm7
E Phrygian modal scale:	Em7	Fmaj7	G7	Am7	Bm7$\flat$5	Cmaj7	Dm7
A$\sharp$ Phrygian modal scale:	A$\sharp$m7	Bmaj7	C$\sharp$7	D$\sharp$m7	E$\sharp$m7$\flat$5	F$\sharp$maj7	G$\sharp$m7
B$\flat$ Phrygian modal scale:	B$\flat$m7	C$\flat$maj7	D$\flat$7	E$\flat$m7	Fm7$\flat$5	G$\flat$maj7	A$\flat$m7

By using this formula you can find out which major 7th, minor 7th, dominant 7th and minor 7th $\flat$5 chords are formed from any Phrygian modal scale.

Note that the chords in the Phrygian modal scale are numbered in comparison to the chords in the major scale with the same keynote. The flat sign before the chords built on the second, third, sixth and seventh degrees show that the roots of these chords are a half step (semitone) lower than the roots of the corresponding chords from the major scale with the same keynote.

Chord progressions using Phrygian harmony

There are no strict 'rules' for constructing chord progressions using Phrygian harmony, but creating a Phrygian chord progression is best achieved by using a combination of chords that most clearly define the particular sound of the Phrygian modal scale. The Im7 chord needs to be used as this establishes both the key centre and the minor tonality. However, other minor keys also have the same minor 7th key chord, so this alone will not establish that the key is Phrygian. The note that distinguishes Phrygian harmony from other minor harmony is the second degree of the scale; the Phrygian modal scale has a flattened (minor) 2nd, whilst both the natural minor scale and the Dorian modal scale have a major 2nd. Using chords that contain this note will therefore establish that the harmony is from the Phrygian modal scale.

For example, here are the three scales starting from an E keynote:

E Phrygian modal scale:	E F G A B C D E
E Dorian modal scale:	E F$\sharp$ G A B C$\sharp$ D E
E natural minor scale:	E F$\sharp$ G A B C D E

Here are the three scales with the chords that can be built on each degree:

E Phrygian modal scale:	Em7	Fmaj7	G7	Am7	Bm7♭5	Cmaj7	Dm7
E Dorian modal:	Em7	F♯m7	Gmaj7	A7	Bm7	C♯m7♭5	Dmaj7
E natural minor scale:	Em7	F♯m7♭5	Gmaj7	Am7	Bm7	Cmaj7	D7

The Fmaj7, Dm7 and Bm7♭5 chords all contain the note F and would therefore be good chord choices for establishing the E Phrygian tonality. The G7 also contains the note F, however care should be taken when using this chord to ensure that the effect of a V – I cadence in C major (G7-C) isn't created. This can be avoided by following it with a chord other than C. Other chords belonging to the Phrygian modal scale can also be used and you should experiment to find combinations that you like.

Here are two examples of Phrygian chord progressions to help you get started.

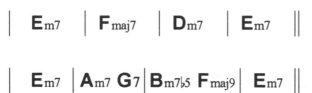

Improvisation using the Phrygian modal scale

Analyse the chords in the progression to assess which key they stem from; begin by assuming that the first chord is the key chord. If this chord is minor then the Phrygian modal scale may be a possible scale choice. However, as other minor scales may also be possible scale choices, the remainder of the chords need to be analysed in order to establish which is the correct scale to use.

For example:

Em7	Bm7♭5	Fmaj9	Dm7 ‖
Im7	Vm7♭5	♭IImaj9	♭VIIm7

Analysis:

i. The progression starts with Em7, thus implying a minor key.

ii. The next chord, Bm7♭5, occurs only in E Phrygian. All the other minor scales you are required to know for Grade Seven contain an F♯ note, whereas both E Phrygian and Bm7♭5 contain an F♮.

iii. Similarly the Fmaj9 and Dm7 chords also contain an F♮ note, confirming E Phrygian modal scale as the best choice.

Improvisation using the whole tone scale

The whole tone scale is used over various *altered* chords, but it is most commonly used in improvisation over dominant 7th ♯5 chords. This is because the notes of the whole tone scale contain the notes of several dominant 7th ♯5 chords.

For example, the C whole tone scale, which contains the notes C D E F♯ G♯ B♭ generates C7♯5, D7♯5, E7♯5, F♯7♯5, G♯7♯5 and B♭7♯5 chords (although the enharmonic spelling may differ). In addition, in jazz-based styles, the whole tone scale is sometimes used over any dominant 7th chord, particularly if the fifth of the chord is omitted by the rhythm section, where it is used as an alternative scale choice to the Mixolydian modal scale or blues scale. The whole tone scale also fits well over dominant 7th ♭5 chords. As with any scale the most important consideration is whether it produces an effective and suitable musical effect.

changing key

In popular music changes of key can occur through simply 'shifting' to a new key or through modulation. For the Grade Seven exam you are required to:

1. construct and identify chord progressions that shift to keys which are near the original key – specifically up or down a whole step (whole tone) or a half step (semitone);

2. construct and identify chord progressions that modulate to keys which are related to the original key.

Shifting to a near key

Keys that are described as *near* the original key are ones which are a whole step or half step away from it.

For example, keys that are *near* to C major are:

D major (a whole step above);

Bb major (a whole step below);

Db major (a half step above);

B major (a half step below).

In popular music, where a key changes by moving up or down by a whole or half step, the chord progression often 'shifts' straight to the new key and repeats the original chord progression in the new key. For example, at the end of a song, the chorus is often repeated in the key a whole or half step above the original key in order to give a 'lift' to the tune.

The following chord progression in C minor is repeated up a half step in the new key of C# minor.

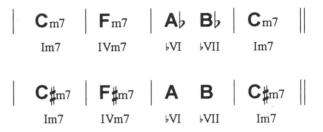

Sometimes the key shift can be 'prepared' by using the dominant seventh chord of the new key. For example, in the following chord progression the key shifts up a half step, from E major to F major, via the use of C7 (the dominant 7th in F major).

	E	A	E	E	A	A	E	B7 C7
E major	I	IV	I	I	IV	IV	I	V7
F major								V7

	F	Bb	F	F	Bb	Bb	F	C7 F
F major	I	IV	I	I	IV	IV	I	V7 I

Modulating to related keys

Keys that are described as *related* to the original key are:

- the *dominant* key – the key (major or minor) which is built on the fifth degree of the original key;

- the *subdominant* – the key (major or minor) which is built on the fourth degree of the original key;

- the *relative minor* or *relative major* – keys that share the same key signature. (The relative minor key is a half step and one whole step below its relative major key.)

- the *tonic minor* or *tonic major* – keys that use the same keynote.

Here are the keys which are *related* to C major

- Dominant (major)   G major
- Dominant (minor)   G minor
- Subdominant (major)   F major
- Subdominant (minor)   F minor
- Relative minor   A minor
- Tonic minor   C minor

Here are the keys which are *related* to A minor

- Dominant (major)   E major
- Dominant (minor)   E minor
- Subdominant (major)   D major
- Subdominant (minor)   D minor
- Relative major   C major
- Tonic major   A major

Modulation is the process of changing from one key to another key, and usually the chord progression in the new key is not the same as that of the original key.

One very effective method of modulating to a related key is to use a *pivot* chord (or chords). A *pivot* chord is one that occurs in both the original and the new key. For example, the following chord progression modulates from C major to G major (the dominant of C). The Em7 and Am7 chords are used as pivot chords as they belong to both the key of C major and the key of G major. Using a pivot chord in this way will ensure that the modulation from one key to another sounds smooth and natural.

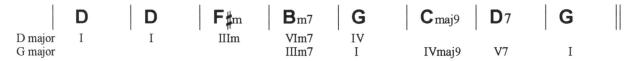

	C	**C**	**F**maj7	**F**maj7	**E**m7	**A**m7	**D**7	**G**	
C major	I	I	IVmaj7	IVmaj7	IIIm7	VIm7			
G major					VIm7	IIm7	V7	I	

The new key of G major is firmly established by following the Am7 chord with harmony that is clearly from the key of G major i.e. V7 – I (D7 – G)

Here are some other examples:

1) The following chord progression modulates from the key of D major to the key of G major (the subdominant of D) using Bm7 and G as the pivot chords.

	D	**D**	**F**♯m	**B**m7	**G**	**C**maj9	**D**7	**G**	
D major	I	I	IIIm	VIm7	IV				
G major				IIIm7	I	IVmaj9	V7	I	

2) The following chord progression modulates from the key of E minor to the key of B minor (the dominant of E minor) using Gmaj7 as the pivot chord.

	Em7	**A**m11	**E**m7	**A**m11	**G**maj7	**A**7	**E**m	**A**	**B**m7	
E minor	Im7	IVm11	Im7	IVm11	♭IIImaj7					
B minor					♭VImaj7	♭VII7	IVm	♭VII	Im7	

3) The following chord progression modulates from the key of F major to the key of D minor (the relative minor). As all the chords in F major are the same as the chords taken from the D natural minor scale, the new key is established by 'borrowing' the V7 chord from D harmonic minor (A7) in order to create a strong V7 – I cadence in D minor.

	F	**B**♭maj7	**G**m7	**C**9	**D**m7	**G**m9	**A**7	**D**m7	
F major	I	IVmaj7	IIm7	V9	VIm7	IIm9			
D minor					Im7	IVm9	V7	Im7	

Improvising over chord progressions that change key

When improvising over chord progressions that contain key changes the principles of identifying the key centres described above still apply.

1) Begin by identifying the starting key, then look at each bar in turn to check that each chord fits into the initial key.

2) When you come across a chord that is no longer in the first key, a key change may have occurred.

3) From this point onwards follow exactly the same procedure as before to identify the new key centre.

4) Do not be misled by chord extensions and variations or passing chords – the key will only have changed if a group of two or more chords establish a new key. Bear in mind that key changes may involve changing to, or between, modal 'keys'.

Example 1:

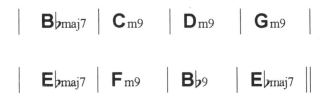

| Gm7 | Gm7 | Cm11 | F7 |

| Gm11 | B♭maj7 | D7 | Gm11 |

| G♯m7 | G♯m7 | C♯m11 | F♯7 |

| G♯m11 | Bmaj7 | D♯7 | G♯m11 ‖

The G natural minor or G pentatonic minor scales would be good scale choices for the first eight bars. The chord progression is then repeated in G♯ minor for the next eight bars, so the G♯ natural minor or G♯ pentatonic minor scales would be good scale choices. Do not be misled by the D7 in the seventh bar or the D♯7 in the penultimate bar. Both of these chords have simply been 'borrowed' from the appropriate harmonic minor scale in order to create a strong V – I cadence in the minor key.

Example 2:

| B♭maj7 | Cm9 | Dm9 | Gm9 |

| E♭maj7 | Fm9 | B♭9 | E♭maj7 ‖

The B♭ major or B♭ pentatonic major scales would work well over the first five chords, as they are all built from the key of B♭ major, however the Gm9 and E♭maj7 chords are being used as pivot chords to modulate into the new key of E♭. It would therefore also be possible to improvise over these two chords using the E♭ major or E♭ pentatonic major scale. The first chord that doesn't belong to both keys is Fm9 (the chord in the key of B♭ major would be an F9 chord) and this is then followed by a V – I cadence (B♭9 – E♭maj7) in E♭ major. The E♭ major or E♭ pentatonic major scale would therefore be good scale choices for the last three or four bars.

Example 3:

| Em7 | Am9 | F♯m7♭5 | B7 |

| Am9 | D9 | Gmaj7 Cmaj7 | Gmaj7 ‖

The E natural minor or E pentatonic minor scales would work well over the first four chords, which are being used to create a chord progression in the key of E minor. (The B7 chord has been 'borrowed' from the E harmonic minor scale to create a strong V – I cadence.) The Am9 is being used as a pivot chord to modulate into the relative major key of G major – it is therefore possible to use either the E natural minor or E pentatonic minor scales or the G major or G pentatonic major scales to improvise over this chord. The movement from D9 to Gmaj7 however clearly indicates a V – I cadence in G major, therefore the G major or G pentatonic major scales are the appropriate scale choices.

For the more advanced player, particularly in a jazz-based style, the use of modal scales could be used to enhance different chord changes. Also, the use of the V chord from the harmonic minor could be reflected by the use of chord tones taken from that scale.

harmonising melodies using chord symbols

The first step to harmonising a melody is to establish which key it is in. In the exam you can use the following methods to work out which key a melody is written in, however in a practical situation it is also essential to learn to listen to the melody's overall sound.

1) Major, natural minor and blues keys all use key signatures. If the tune is written using the blues scale the melody will also use accidentals to create the flattened third, fifth and seventh. In most simple melodies, major and natural minor keys are unlikely to use accidentals in the melody, so you can identify whether the key is major, natural minor or blues by seeing which, if any, accidentals are used.

2) If the melody doesn't contain any accidentals the next step is to identify whether it is in a major or minor key. This can be achieved by seeing which note the tonality of the melody is based around: often the melody will begin or end on the keynote. For example, if the melody has four flats in the key signature, and resolves around the note of A♭, it is likely to be in A♭ major; if it resolves around the note of F it is likely to be in F minor.

3) In popular music, if the melody uses both a key signature and accidentals it is likely to be in a blues key. By identifying which notes have been flattened it is then possible to work out in which blues key the melody is written. For example, if the key signature has three sharps and uses accidentals in the melody to produce the notes C♮, E♭ and G♮, then it is likely that the melody is written using the A blues scale.

4) If the melody is written without a key signature but uses accidentals then it is likely to be written using a modal scale. By seeing which accidentals are used, and which note the tonality of the melody is based around, it is possible to work out which modal scale is being used. For example, if the accidentals in the melody include E♭ and B♭ and the melody ends on C, it is likely to be written using the C Dorian modal scale.

Once you have established the key you then need to work out the chords that are in the key (as explained earlier in this chapter).

There are many different ways of harmonising melodies, and depending upon the intended effect, the notes of a melody are certainly not always restricted to the chord tones of the accompanying chords. However, to ensure unambiguous analysis, we suggest that in the exam you *do* regard notes of the melody mainly as chord tones, and base your choice of chords on this premise.

You should also bear in mind the other suggestions that we have previously made for writing effective chord progressions.

Here are some examples of melodies harmonised using chord symbols. The chords used are only one possible way of harmonising the melody, and various other chord options may be musically effective.

D major melody and chords

F# minor melody and chords

Bb blues melody and chords

B Dorian melody and chords

grade eight

In addition to the requirements for Grade Seven, at Grade Eight you are also required to:

- construct and analyse chord progressions involving modulation to any key;

- analyse chord progressions which use non-diatonic chords;

- use chord symbols to harmonise a melody that may modulate to any near or related key;

- apply scales and modal scales from Section 1 in improvisation, including recognising modulations to any key.

changing key

For the Grade Eight exam you are required to identify and construct chord sequences that change key (i.e. modulate). The modulation may be from any key to any other key, and more than one key change may occur or be requested.

In some popular music chord progressions a change of key may only occur briefly before the chords return to the original key (known as a *transitory* key change), however, for the purposes of the exam, all key changes will be ones which clearly establish the new key. This also applies to chord progressions that you are required to write.

There are various ways of changing key, most commonly using pivot chord modulation (as explained for Grade Seven). However, modulation can also occur by using a chord that is *not* common to both keys (known as *direct* modulation). Even in this instance, the two chords that bridge the two keys may often have a note in common and frequently there is a chromatic link which helps make the key change less abrupt.

A common composition technique involving direct modulation is to use the dominant seventh chord of the new key, to 'prepare' the listener for the key change that is about to take place.

For example, the following chord progression modulates from the key of E♭ major to the key of G major by way of a D7 chord; it then modulates back to E♭ major by way of a B♭7 chord.

		E♭	B♭	Cm11	A♭maj7	E♭maj7	B♭7	Dm7♭5	D7	
E♭ major		I	V	VIm11	IVmaj7	Imaj7	V7	VIIm7♭5		
G major									V7	

		G	D7	Cmaj7	Gmaj7	Am7	C	Bm7	B♭7	
E♭ major									V7	
G major		I	V7	IVmaj7	Imaj7	IIm7	IV	IIIm7		

		E♭maj7	Gm7	A♭	E♭	
E♭ major		Imaj7	IIIm7	IV	I	

harmonising melodies that change key

To harmonise melodies that change key you should use the same basic principles as described previously in Grade Seven, but at Grade Eight you will also need to identify where a melody has changed key and into which key it has moved. The occurance of accidentals will help you identify the new key signature.

Here are two examples of melodies that have changed key, harmonised using chord symbols. (The chords used are only suggestions and other possibilities exist.)

This melody modulates to the subdominant of the original key – i.e. from A major to D major.

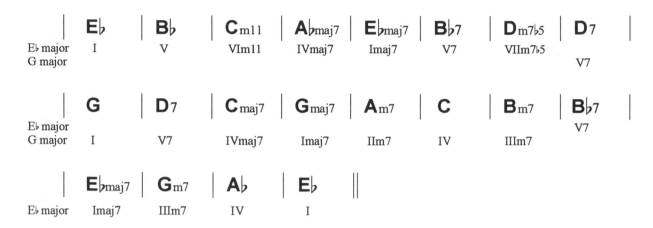

This melody modulates down a whole step – i.e. from C minor down to B♭ minor.

applying scales to improvisation

The additional scales which are set for the Grade Eight exam are:

- Locrian modal scale
- Phrygian major modal scale
- Jazz melodic minor scale
- Lydian ♭7 modal scale (also known as the 'Lydian dominant' scale).
- Altered scale
- Diminished scale

These scales are not generally used to create chord progressions using their own harmony, instead they are mainly used over specific chords or (particularly in jazz-based music) to provide alternative sounds to more commonly used scales.

Locrian modal scale

The Locrian modal scale is most commonly used over minor 7th ♭5 chords, as this is the key chord of the modal scale. It is often used to create a dissonant 'diminished' tonality in a piece of music.

Phrygian major modal scale

The key chord of the Phrygian major modal scale is a dominant 7th chord so the Phrygian major modal scale is often used in music that uses dominant 7th chords. It is a particularly good scale choice for using over dominant 7th ♭9 chords as the second note of the scale (♭2) creates the ♭9th chord extension.

For example, the C Phrygian major modal scale contains the notes of the C7♭9 chord:

C	D♭	E	F	G	A♭	B♭	C		C	E	G	B♭	D♭
1	♭2	3	4	5	♭6	♭7	8		1	3	5	♭7	♭9

The Phrygian major modal scale is also often used over 5th 'power chords' and is typically used in rock-based music as an alternative to the Mixolydian modal scale or the blues scale.

Jazz melodic minor

The jazz melodic minor scale can be used as an alternative to the harmonic minor over minor/major 7th chords, as this is the key chord of the scale. The scale is sometimes used in jazz-based music as an alternative Improvisation tool to the more obvious minor scales.

Lydian ♭7 modal scale

The key chord of the Lydian ♭7 modal scale is a dominant 7th chord so the Lydian ♭7 modal scale is another scale which is used in music that uses dominant 7th chords, as an alternative to the Mixolydian modal scale or the blues scale. It is a particularly good scale choice for using over dominant 7th #11 chords as the fourth note of the scale (#4) creates the #11 chord extension.

For example, the C Lydian ♭7 modal scale contains the notes of the C7#11 chord:

C	D	E	F#	G	A	B♭		C	E	G	B♭	F#
1	2	3	#4	5	6	♭7		1	3	5	♭7	#11

The altered scale

The altered scale is an additional scale that can be used over dominant 7th chords, and music based on dominant harmony, as its key chord is also a dominant 7th chord. It is particularly appropriate to use this scale over dominant 7th #5 chords, especially if they also contain the ♭9, #9 or #11 altered chord extensions.

For example, the C altered scale contains the notes of the C7#5 ♭9/#9/#11 chord:

C	D♭	D#	E	F#	G#	B♭		C	E	G#	B♭	D♭	D#	F#
1	♭2	#2	3	#4	#5	♭7		1	3	#5	♭7	♭9	#9	#11

The diminished scale

The whole/half diminished scale can be used over diminished triads and diminished seventh chords. For example, the whole/half diminished scale starting on C contains the notes C D E♭ F G♭ A♭ B♭♭ and B and therefore the notes of the C° triad and C°7 chord.

The half/whole diminished scale can be used over dominant 7th chords as the notes of the dominant 7th chord are contained within the scale. For example, the half/whole diminished scale starting on C contains the notes C D♭ D# E F# G A B♭ and therefore includes the notes of the C7 chord (C E G B♭).

Because of the 'symmetrical' nature of the diminished scale it has a very strong 'internal' sound that can be used to introduce non-diatonic notes though playing 'patterns' based on the notes of the scale.

We recommend that in order to understand the use of these scales in improvisation you experiment with them in a wide variety of musical contexts.

analysing chord progressions that use non-diatonic chords

Chord progressions sometimes contain chords that do not 'belong' to the key. These chords are described as *non-diatonic* as they contain notes which are not contained in the key scale. Non-diatonic chords are identified by using the appropriate Roman Numerals.

Non-diatonic dominant 7th chords

Blues-based music uses many non-diatonic chords, as described previously, in particular dominant 7th chords on the 1st and 4th degrees. In other styles of popular music, the most commonly used non-diatonic chords are when the minor chords from the 2nd, 3rd and 6th degrees of the major scale are changed to major triads or dominant 7th chords.

In the following chord progression the chord built on the sixth degree (bar three) has been changed to a dominant 7th (non-diatonic) chord. (In a diatonic major chord progression the chord built on the sixth degree is a minor 7th chord.) This change, to a non-diatonic chord, is identified by describing the chord as VI7 rather than VIm7.

Amaj7	**C#**m7	**F#**7	**B**m7 **E**7
Imaj7	IIIm7	VI7	IIm7 V7

In the next chord sequence the chord built on the second degree (bar three, first chord) has been changed to a dominant 7th (non-diatonic) chord. (In a diatonic major chord progression the chord built on the second degree is a minor 7th chord.) This change to a non-diatonic chord is identified by describing the chord as II7 rather than IIm7.

B♭maj7	**E♭**maj7	**C**7 **F**7	**B♭**
Imaj7	IVmaj7	II7 V7	I

Non-diatonic chords from the natural minor scale

Other common non-diatonic chords used in major keys are chords which are 'borrowed' from the natural minor scale.

Here are some examples of chord sequences which have 'borrowed' chords from the natural minor scale. The Roman Numerals which identify the chords describe the chord type and the interval from the keynote.

The following chord sequence is mainly in G major, but the chords in the last two bars (♭VImaj7 and ♭VII7) are 'borrowed' from the G natural minor scale.

G **C**maj7	**B**m7	**E**♭maj7	**F**7
I IVmaj7	IIIm7	♭VImaj7	♭VII7

In the next example the chord sequence is mainly in B♭ major, but in bars five and six the two chords (IVm7 and ♭IIImaj7) are 'borrowed' from the B♭ natural minor scale.

B♭maj7	**C**m9	**F**7	**G**m7	**E**♭m7	**D**♭maj7	**C**m7	**F**9
Imaj7	IIm9	V7	VIm7	IVm7	♭IIImaj7	IIm7	V9

Diminished 7th chords

There are no fixed 'rules' as to where diminished 7th chords can be used in popular music chord progressions, however they most often appear as a 'link' chord joining two diatonic chords chromatically. For example, in the following chord sequence C♯°7 is used to link Cmaj7 and Dm7 (chords I and II in C major).

Cmaj7	**C**♯°7	**D**m7	**G**7
Imaj7	♯I°7	IIm7	V7

The diminished 7th chord is also commonly used as a ♯IV°7 chord as in the next example.

Here a G♯°7 chord is used to link G and D/A (chords IV and I in the key of D major).

D	**G** **G**♯°7	**D/A** **A**7	**D**maj7
I	IV ♯IV°7	I V7	Imaj7

Minor/major 7th chords

Minor/major 7th chords (which are derived from the harmonic minor scale) can be thought of as a variation of a minor 7th chord. Although they can be used in other situations, they are most commonly used to create a chromatic effect within a chord progression. For example:

Fm	**F**m/maj7	**F**m7	**F**m/maj7	**F**m
Im	Im/maj7	Im7	Im/maj7	Im

Altered chords

Using a chord that contains an altered (♭/♯) 5th or altered extension (e.g. ♭/♯9) does not, in most situations, fundamentally change the function of that chord. Consequently, altered chords are often used as a method of making a chord progression sound more interesting – particularly in jazz-based styles. Careful use of altered chords can also enable a smoother transition to the next chord in a progression. We recommend that you experiment with a wide range of altered chords when practising writing chord progressions in order to explore a full variety of harmonic possibilities.

When using Roman numerals to describe altered chords, the chord type should be described in full.

For example:

C7 **C**7♯5	**F**7 **G**7♯9	**C**7
I7 I7♯5	IV7 V7♯9	I7

There follows some examples of the types of questions that candidates may be asked in this section of the exam. If you can't answer a question, then carefully re-read the preceding chapter and, if necessary, refer to the earlier books in the series.

Sample questions for Grade Six

Q1.   Name the scale from which all of the following chords can be derived, and identify the chords using Roman Numerals.

A1.   Scale _____

| Dm7 | G7 | Em7 | Am9 | |

   ____   ____   ____   ____

| Dm7 | Fmaj7 | Am | Dm7 | ||

   ____   ____   ____   ____

Q2.   Using at least five different chords, write an eight bar chord progression in the key of Db major. Include a IV-I (plagal) cadence and one other common cadential chord movement. Identify both the cadences by writing the appropriate Roman Numerals below them.

A2. | | | | |

     | | | | ||

Q3.   Using at least five different chords, write an eight bar chord progression that could be used as a backing for an improvisation using the A Lydian modal scale.

A3. | | | | |

     | | | | ||

Q4.   Name a scale that could be used for improvising over the following chord progression.

| E7 | Dmaj9 | G#m7b5 | E9 | |

A4.   _____

Q5.   Describe how you might use the chromatic scale in an improvisation.

A5.   _____

_____

Q1. Harmonise the following melody using chord symbols.

A1.

Q2. Indicate the possible scale choices that could be used to improvise over the following chord sequence, writing under the bars which scales could be used.

| Bm7   E7 | Bm9   E9 | Cm7   F7 | Cm9   F9 |

A2. _____

| Bm7   E7 | Amaj7 | F#m7   E9 | A6 ||

_____

Q3. Write an eight bar chord progression using at least four different chords, which could be used as a backing for an improvisation using the B Phrygian modal scale.

A3. | | | | |

     | | | | ||

Q4. Using at least seven different chords, write a 16 bar chord progression that starts in the key of A♭ major and modulates to the relative minor key. Include four common cadential movements – identifying these when they occur.

A4. | | | | |

     | | | | |

     | | | | |

     | | | | ||

Sample Questions for Grade Eight

Q1. Harmonise the following melody using chord symbols.

A1.
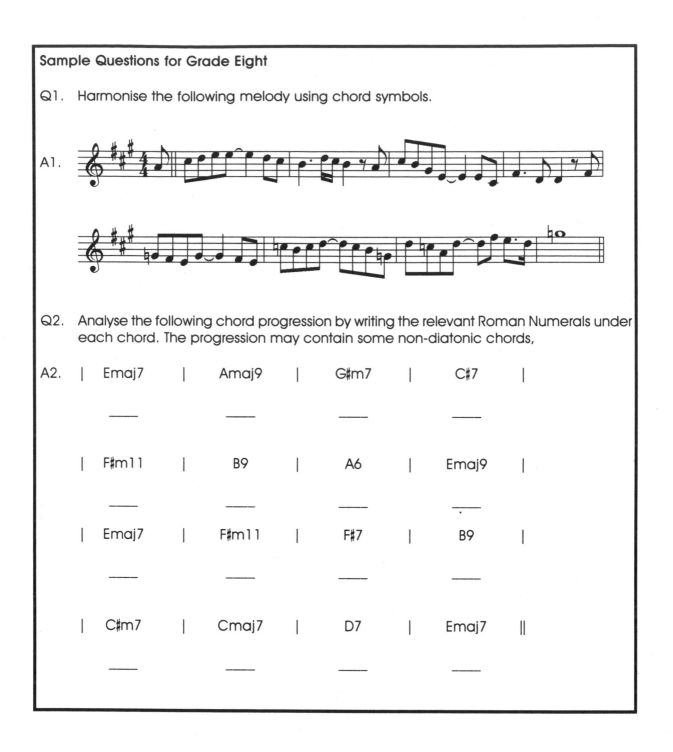

Q2. Analyse the following chord progression by writing the relevant Roman Numerals under each chord. The progression may contain some non-diatonic chords,

A2. | Emaj7 | Amaj9 | G#m7 | C#7 |

      ——————   ——————   ——————   ——————

    | F#m11 | B9 | A6 | Emaj9 |

      ——————   ——————   ——————   ——————

    | Emaj7 | F#m11 | F#7 | B9 |

      ——————   ——————   ——————   ——————

    | C#m7 | Cmaj7 | D7 | Emaj7 ||

      ——————   ——————   ——————   ——————

Q3. Explain how EACH of the following scales could be used in an improvisation – suggesting a chord type over which each scale can be used.

A3. a) Locrian modal scale

_____

b) Phrygian major modal scale

_____

c) Lydian ♭7 modal scale

_____

d) altered scale

_____

e) whole/half diminished scale

_____

Q4. Using at least one different chord per bar, write a 16 bar chord progression starting in the key of C minor that includes at least two cadences and two modulations. Identify the cadences and modulations when they occur.

A4. | | | | |

| | | | |

| | | | |

| | | | ||

Section six – transposition

In this section of the exam you will be asked to demonstrate your skills in transposing chord progressions and melodies.

Transposition requirements for Grade Six

- Transposing chords, presented in chord symbols, into any key within a range of keys up to 5 sharps and 5 flats.

- Transposing melodies up or down a whole step (whole tone) within a range of keys up to 5 sharps and 5 flats.

Transposition requirements for Grade Seven

- Transposing chords, presented in chord symbols, into any key.

- Transposing melodies into near or related keys.

- Transposing between the treble and bass clef.

Transposition requirements for Grade Eight

- Transposing chords, presented in chord symbols, into any key.

- Transposing melodies into any key.

- Transposing between the treble and bass clef.

---

the theory

transposing chords

Here are two different methods that you can use to transpose chord progressions. Both methods will give exactly the same result. In both instances, make sure that you use the correct enharmonic spelling for the new key – particularly when transposing from a sharp key to a flat key (or vice versa).

chord numbers

Identify the key of the original chord progression and the chord numbers for each of the chords. Then, using the chord numbers, work out the chords in the new key.

For example, to transpose the following chord progression into the key of D major, the first step is to identify the key of the progression.

| B_{maj7} | $D\sharp_{m7}$ $G\sharp_{m9}$ | $C\sharp_{m7}$ $F\sharp_9$ | B_{maj7} ‖

The above chord progression is in the key of B major because:

- the progression starts and ends on a B major 7th chord.

- all the chords are in the key of B major.

- the movement of F#9 to Bmaj7 forms a V-I (perfect) cadence in the key of B major.

Having worked out the key of the progression next identify the key chord – which will have the chord number 'I'. From this, the other chord numbers can then be worked out. You can check that you have worked them out correctly by ensuring that the chord type for each degree corresponds to the standard pattern of chords for the key.

The chord numbers for the above progression are:

| Imaj7 | IIIm7   VIm9 | IIm7   V9 | Imaj7 ‖

To transpose the chord progression into D major, you need to work out what the Imaj7, IIIm7, VIm9, IIm7, and V9 chords are, in the key of D major. Remember, the chord quality for each chord is the same as in the original key – therefore the chord progression transposed into the key of D major will be:

| D maj7 | F#m7 | Bm9 | Em7 | A9 | Dmaj7 |

The same principle applies when transposing between two minor keys, the only difference being that chords should be numbered according to their position in the pattern of chords built from the appropriate minor scale.

intervals

Another way to transpose the chord progression is to change the root note of each chord by the required interval. You work this out, by first identifying what the original key is, as above, and then by working out what interval is created between the key chords of both keys. This will determine the interval you

need to move each chord (either up or down). In this instance, D is a minor 3rd above B, so for this transposition, the root note of each chord needs to be moved up an interval of a minor third. As in the previous method, the chord types stay the same as in the original key.

- Bmaj7 would move up a minor 3rd interval to become Dmaj7.

- D#m7 would move up a minor 3rd interval to become F#m7.

- G#m9 would move up a minor 3rd interval to become Bm9.

- C#m7 would move up a minor 3rd interval to become Em7.

- F#9 would move up a minor 3rd interval to become A9.

The same method can be used to transpose between two minor keys.

transposing melodies

Here are two methods that you can use for transposing melodies:

scale spellings

Identify the key of the melody, by observing the key signature and any accidentals contained within the melody. The appropriate scale and scale spelling can then be identified. Then, using the scale spelling work out the notes of the scale in the new key.

In the following example, the key of the melody is E major, as there are four sharps in the key signature and the melody begins and ends on E.

The scale spelling for the major scale is 1 2 3 4 5 6 7 8. Therefore, each note of the melody can be identified as follows:

To transpose the melody into the key of D major (i.e. down one whole step / tone), you need to work out which notes these scale numbers would refer to in the key of D, remembering to use the correct key signature for the new key.

To ensure that you have transposed the melody correctly, including writing the notes in the appropriate octave, check that the 'shape' of the transposed melody follows the shape of the original melody. For instance, notice that the penultimate note in this example, whilst given the scale number '7', is in fact in a lower octave.

The same principles can be applied when transposing between two minor keys, the only difference being that the notes should be numbered according to their position in, and the scale spelling of, the appropriate minor scale. The example below shows transposition from the key of A minor to B minor.

intervals

Another way to transpose the melody, whether in a major or minor key, is to change each note by the required interval. You work this out, by first identifying the original key of the melody, as described above. Then, work out what interval is created between the keynote of both keys: this determines the interval that you need to move each note of the melody (either up or down). For example, when transposing from E major down to D major, D is a whole step (whole tone) below E – so, for this transposition, each note of the melody would need to be moved down a whole step.

To confirm that the transposition is correct, check that the 'shape' of the transposed melody follows the shape of the original melody – ensuring that the intervals between each note and the next are the same as in the original melody. Remember to use the correct key signature for the new key.

grade six

For the Grade Six exam you may be asked to transpose chord sequences into any key within a range of keys up to 5 sharps and 5 flats. You may also be asked to transpose melodies up or down a whole step (whole tone) within the same range of keys. The preceding information in this chapter explains how to undertake such transposition.

grade seven

For the Grade Seven exam you may be asked to transpose chord progressions into *any* key. You may also be asked to transpose melodies up or down into 'near or related' keys (i.e. into a key that is: a whole or half step above or below the original key; the dominant or subdominant of the original key).

The preceding information in this chapter explains how to undertake such transposition. However, at Grade Seven, you may also be asked to transpose melodies between the treble and bass clef (changing the octave when requested).

For example, to transpose this melody down into the key of D major, writing it in the bass clef two octaves below where the transposed melody would be in the treble clef:

- ■ work out the interval between the two keys (in this instance, down a whole step from E major to D major);

- ■ notice where the first note of the transposed melody would be in the treble clef (in this instance, D just below the staff);

- write the new key signature in the bass clef;
- write the melody in the bass clef starting with the 'D' note which is two octaves below where the transposed melody would start in the treble clef. The easiest way to work this out is to think of the notes in relationship to 'middle C' – which is a useful marker point midway between the two staffs.

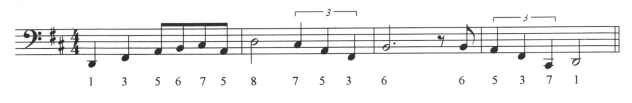

grade eight

In addition to transposing chord progressions (which may contain some non-diatonic chords) into any key, you may also be asked to transpose melodies up or down into *any* key, using the bass and treble clefs (changing the octave when requested). This can be done by using a combination of the methods described above. In order to become fluent in transposition, we recommend that you practise transposing on a regular basis – transposing between the two clefs and between a wide range of keys.

the exam

Below are some examples of the types of questions that candidates may be asked in this section of the exam. If you can't answer a question, then carefully re-read the preceding chapter. Once you've worked through these questions you can check your answers by looking in the back of the book.

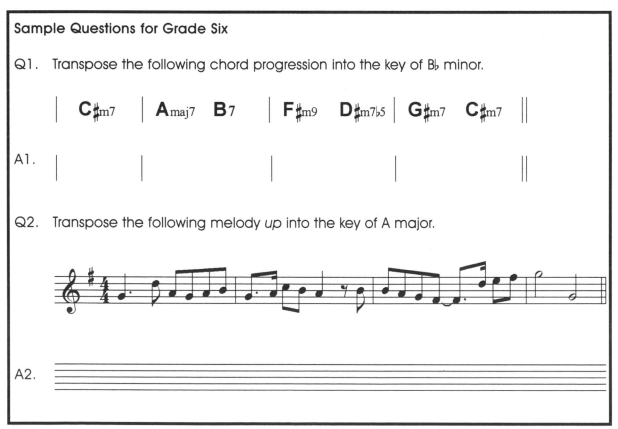

Sample Questions for Grade Six

Q1. Transpose the following chord progression into the key of B♭ minor.

| C♯m7 | Amaj7 B7 | F♯m9 D♯m7♭5 | G♯m7 C♯m7 ‖

A1.

Q2. Transpose the following melody *up* into the key of A major.

A2.

Sample Questions for Grade Seven

Q1. Transpose the following chord progression into the key of F# major.

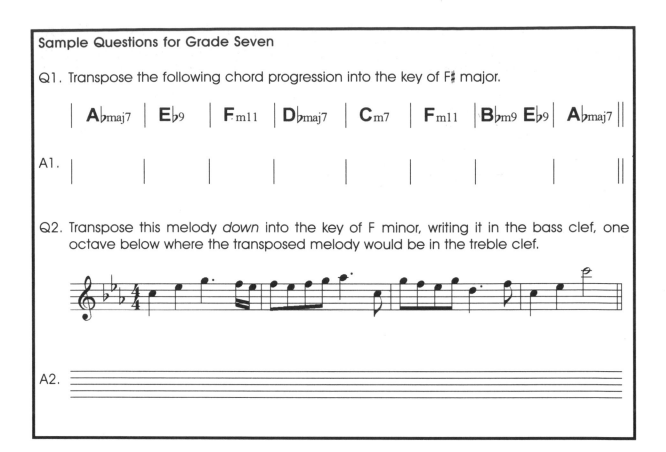

Q2. Transpose this melody *down* into the key of F minor, writing it in the bass clef, one octave below where the transposed melody would be in the treble clef.

A2.

Sample Questions for Grade Eight

Q1. Transpose the following chord progression into the key of E major.

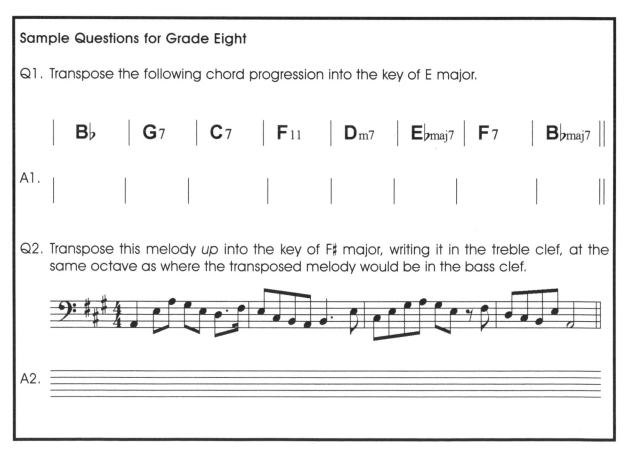

Q2. Transpose this melody *up* into the key of F# major, writing it in the treble clef, at the same octave as where the transposed melody would be in the bass clef.

A2.

Section Seven – Sample answers

Note that all the answers below are 'sample answers' and for several questions there are a range of other answers that would also be acceptable.

Section One – scales and keys [Max. 20 marks]

A1.

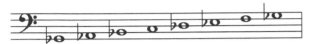

A2.

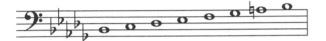

A3.

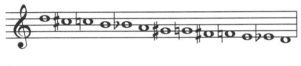

A4.

A5.   Lydian modal scale: 1 2 3 #4 5 6 7 8
      Dorian modal scale: 1 2 ♭3 4 5 6 ♭7 8
      Mixolydian modal scale: 1 2 3 4 5 6 ♭7 8

Section Two – chords [Max. 20 marks]

A1.

A2.

A3.

A4.

A5.

Major 9th: 1 3 5 7 9
Minor 9th: 1 ♭3 5 ♭7 9
Dominant 9th: 1 3 5 ♭7 9

Section Three – rhythm notation [Max. 10 marks]

A1.

A2.

A3.

Section Four – knowledge of popular music [15 marks]

You are required to write an essay of approximately 400 to 500 words in this section of the exam. Marks will be awarded for relevant factual information given in your answer, so you should try to make your essay as comprehensive as possible within the word limit given. You should try to structure your answer so that the information is presented in a clear and focused way. However, you will not be marked on the quality or style of your use of the English language, unless this affects the factual content of your essay.

Section Five – harmony [25 marks]

A1.

Scale: D Dorian modal scale

	Dm7		G7		Em7		Am9	
	Im7		IV7		IIm7		Vm9	

	Dm7		Fmaj7		Am		Dm7	‖
	Im7		♭IIImaj7		Vm		Im7	

A2.

	D♭maj7		E♭m		A♭7		B♭m7	
							V - VI	

	G♭maj9		Fm7		G♭maj9		D♭maj7	‖
					IV - I			

A3.

| Amaj7 | | B9 | | Amaj7 | | G#m7 | |
| C#m7 | | D#m7♭5 | | F#m7 G#m7 | | Amaj7 | ‖ |

A4.

E Mixolydian modal scale

A5.

Notes from the chromatic scale can be used in an improvisation as passing notes to 'link' diatonic notes or phrases.

Section Six – transposition [10 marks]

A1.

A2.

---

grade seven

Section One – scales and keys [Max. 20 marks]

A1.

A2.

A3.

A4.

A5.   Phrygian modal scale: 1 ♭2 ♭3 4 5 ♭6 ♭7 8
Blues scale: 1 ♭3 4 ♭5 5 ♭7 8
Chromatic scale: 1 ♭2 2 ♭3 3 4 #4 5 ♭6 6 ♭7 7 8

Section Two – chords [Max. 20 marks]

A1.

A2.

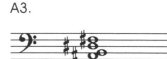

A3.

A4.

A5.

Dominant 11th: 1 3 5 ♭7 9 11
Major 13th: 1 3 5 7 9 11 13
Minor 13th: 1 ♭3 5 ♭7 9 11 13

Section Three – rhythm notation [Max. 10 marks]

A1.

A2.

A3.

Section Four – knowledge of popular music [15 marks]

You are required to write an essay of approximately 400 to 500 words in this section of the exam. Marks will be awarded for relevant factual information given in your answer, so you should try to make your essay as comprehensive as possible within the word limit given. You should try to structure your answer so that the information is presented in a clear and focused way. However, you will not be marked on the quality or style of your use of the English language, unless this affects the factual content of your essay.

Section Five – harmony [25 marks]

A1.

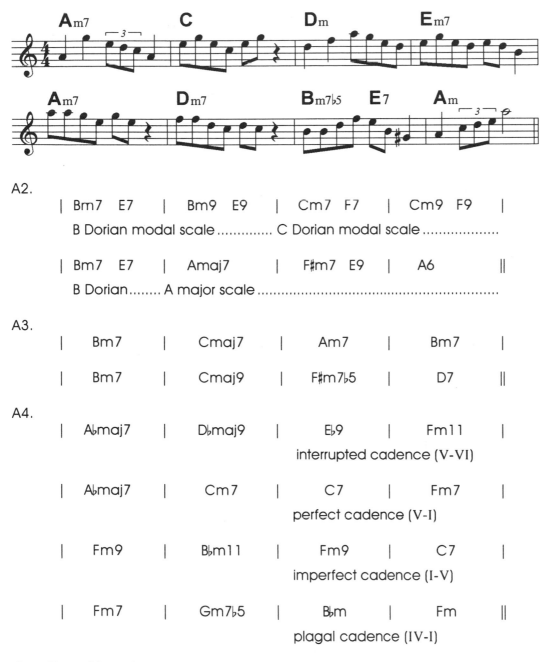

A2.

| Bm7 E7 | Bm9 E9 | Cm7 F7 | Cm9 F9 |

B Dorian modal scale .... C Dorian modal scale ....

| Bm7 E7 | Amaj7 | F#m7 E9 | A6 ||

B Dorian........ A major scale ....

A3.

| Bm7 | Cmaj7 | Am7 | Bm7 |

| Bm7 | Cmaj9 | F#m7♭5 | D7 ||

A4.

| A♭maj7 | D♭maj9 | E♭9 | Fm11 |

interrupted cadence (V-VI)

| A♭maj7 | Cm7 | C7 | Fm7 |

perfect cadence (V-I)

| Fm9 | B♭m11 | Fm9 | C7 |

imperfect cadence (I-V)

| Fm7 | Gm7♭5 | B♭m | Fm ||

plagal cadence (IV-I)

Section Six – transposition [10 marks]

A1.

| F#maj7 | C#9 | D#m11 | Bmaj7 | A#m7 | D#m11 | G#m9 C#9 | F#maj7 ||

A2.

Section One – scales and keys [Max. 20 marks]

A1.

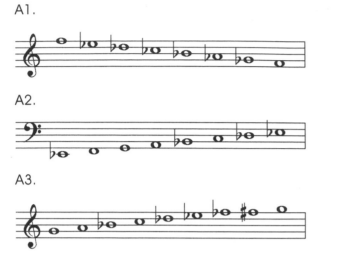

A2.

A3.

A4.

A5.   Locrian modal scale: 1 ♭2 ♭3 4 ♭5 ♭6 ♭7 8
            Phrygian major modal scale: 1 ♭2 3 4 5 ♭6 ♭7 8
            Jazz melodic minor scale: 1 2 ♭3 4 5 6 7 8

Section Two – chords [Max. 20 marks]

A1.

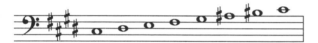

A2.

A3.

A4.

A5.

Dominant 7th ♯9: 1 3 5 ♭7 ♯9
Minor 7th ♭9: 1 ♭3 5 ♭7 ♭9
Dominant 7th ♯11: 1 3 5 ♭7 ♯11

Section Three – rhythm notation *[Max. 10 marks]*

A1.

A2.

A3.

Section Four – knowledge of popular music *[15 marks]*

You are required to write an essay of approximately 400 to 500 words in this section of the exam. Marks will be awarded for relevant factual information given in your answer, so you should try to make your essay as comprehensive as possible within the word limit given. You should try to structure your answer so that the information is presented in a clear and focused way. However, you will not be marked on the quality or style of your use of the English language, unless this affects the factual content of your essay.

Section Five – harmony *[25 marks]*

A1.

A2-4: See overleaf.

A2.

	Emaj7		Amaj9		G#m7		C#7	
	Imaj7		IVmaj9		IIIm7		VI7	

	F#m11		B9		A6		Emaj9	
	IIm11		V9		IV6		Imaj9	

	Emaj7		F#m11		F#7		B9	
	Imaj7		IIm11		II7		V9	

	C#m7		Cmaj7		D7		Emaj7	‖
	VIm7		♭VImaj7		♭VII7		Imaj7	

A3.

a) The Locrian modal scale can be used over minor 7th ♭5 chords.

b) The Phrygian major modal scale can be used over dominant 7th ♭9 chords.

c) The Lydian ♭7 modal scale can be used over dominant 7th ♯11 chords.

d) The altered scale can be used over dominant 7th ♯5 chords.

e) The whole/half diminished scale can be used over diminished 7th chords.

A4.

	Cm		B♭ A♭		Fm11		Cm7 Gm7	
							imperfect cadence (I-V)	

	Cm7		Dm7♭5 A♭		G G7		Cmaj7	
					perfect cadence (V-I) Modulation to C major			

	Cmaj9		Fmaj7		Dm9		Em7	

	E7		Amaj7		Bm7 E7		A	‖
Modulation to A major								

Section Six – transposition *[10 marks]*

A1.

A2.

Examination Entry Form for LCM
Popular Music Theory examination.

GRADES 6, 7 or 8

Please use BLOCK CAPITAL LETTERS when filling out this form

State the examination grade you are entering (6, 7, or 8): _____

Please note: Once you have submitted this form to the Examinations Registry you will be supplied with additional entry forms enabling you to enter either of the other advanced grades. If you need to re-take the same examination a 're-entry form' will be supplied (see overleaf for details).

SESSION (Summer/Winter): _____ YEAR: _____

Preferred Examination Centre (if known): _____
If left blank, you will be examined at the nearest examination centre to your home address.

Candidate Details:

Candidate Name (as to appear on certificate):

_____

Address: _____

_____

_____ Postcode: _____

Tel. No. (day): _____ _____ (evening): _____

Teacher Details:

Teacher Name (as to appear on certificate): _____

Registry Tutor Code (if applicable): _____

Address: _____

_____ Postcode: _____

Tel. No. (day): _____ (evening): _____

The standard LCM entry form is NOT valid for
Popular Music Theory entries. Entry to the examination
is only possible via this original form.

Photocopies of this form will not be accepted under
any circumstances.

IMPORTANT NOTES

- It is the candidate's responsibility to have knowledge of, and comply with, the current syllabus requirements. When a candidate is entered for an examination by a teacher, the teacher must take responsibility that the candidate is entered in accordance with the current syllabus requirements. In particular, from 2005 it is important to check that the contents of this book match the syllabus that is valid at the time of entry.

- For candidates with special needs, a letter giving details should be attached.

- Theory dates are the same worldwide and are fixed annually by LCM. Details of entry deadlines and examination dates are obtainable from the Examinations Registry.

- Submission of this entry is an undertaking to abide by the current regulations as listed in the current syllabus and any subsequent regulations updates published by the LCM / Examinations Registry.

- UK entries should be sent to The Examinations Registry, Registry House, Churchill Mews, Dennett Rd, Croydon, Surrey CR0 3JH.

- Overseas entrants should contact the LCM / Examinations Registry for details of their international representatives.

- Once this form has been submitted, the Examinations Registry will supply the candidate with additional entry forms enabling the candidate to enter either of the other advanced grades. If the candidate wishes to re-take an examination a 're-entry form' will be supplied, free of charge, upon receipt of a letter of request and a copy of original examination report form.

Examination Fee   £ _____

Late Entry Fee (if applicable)   £ _____

Total amount submitted: £ _____

Cheques or postal orders should be made payable to The Examinations Registry.
Entries cannot be made by credit card.

A current list of fees is available from the Examinations Registry.

The Examinations Registry
Registry House
Churchill Mews
Dennett Road
Croydon
Surrey, U.K.
CR0 3JH

Tel: 020 8665 7666
Fax: 020 8665 7667
Email: mail@ExamRegistry.com